Heart of Africa

Coloring Book

Lions

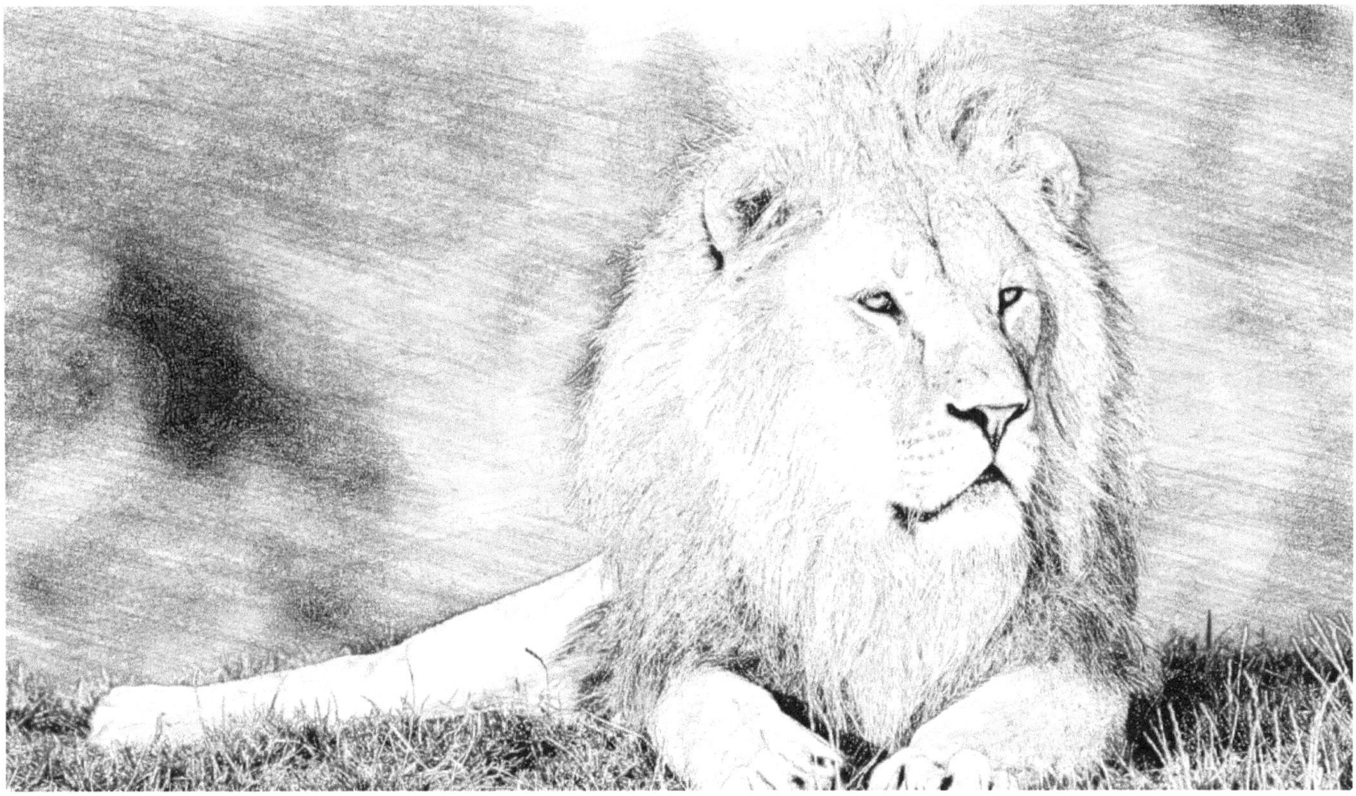

R.D. Jentsch

Texas

ISBN 978-1515361947

Dedicated to
My Family & My Best Friend

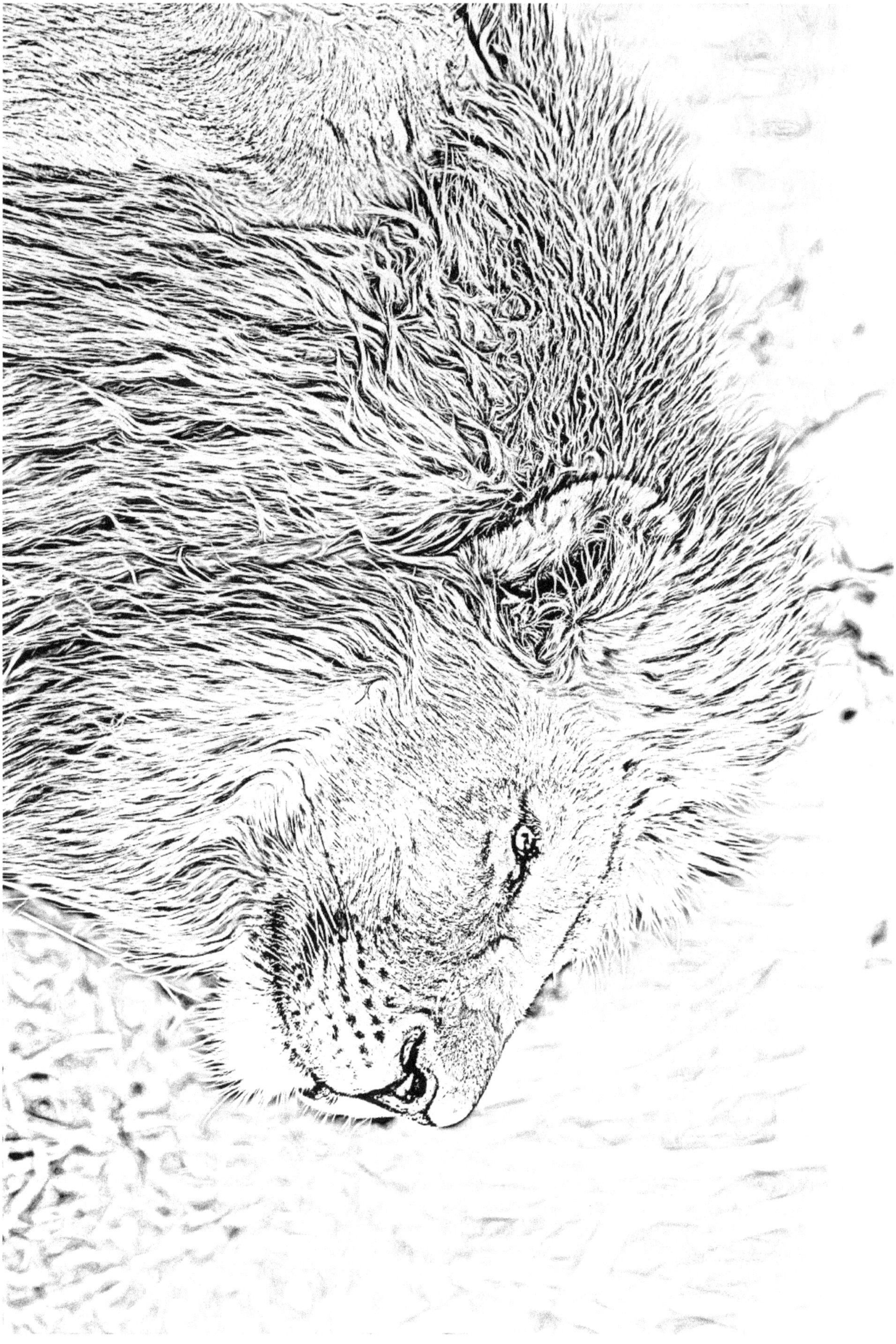

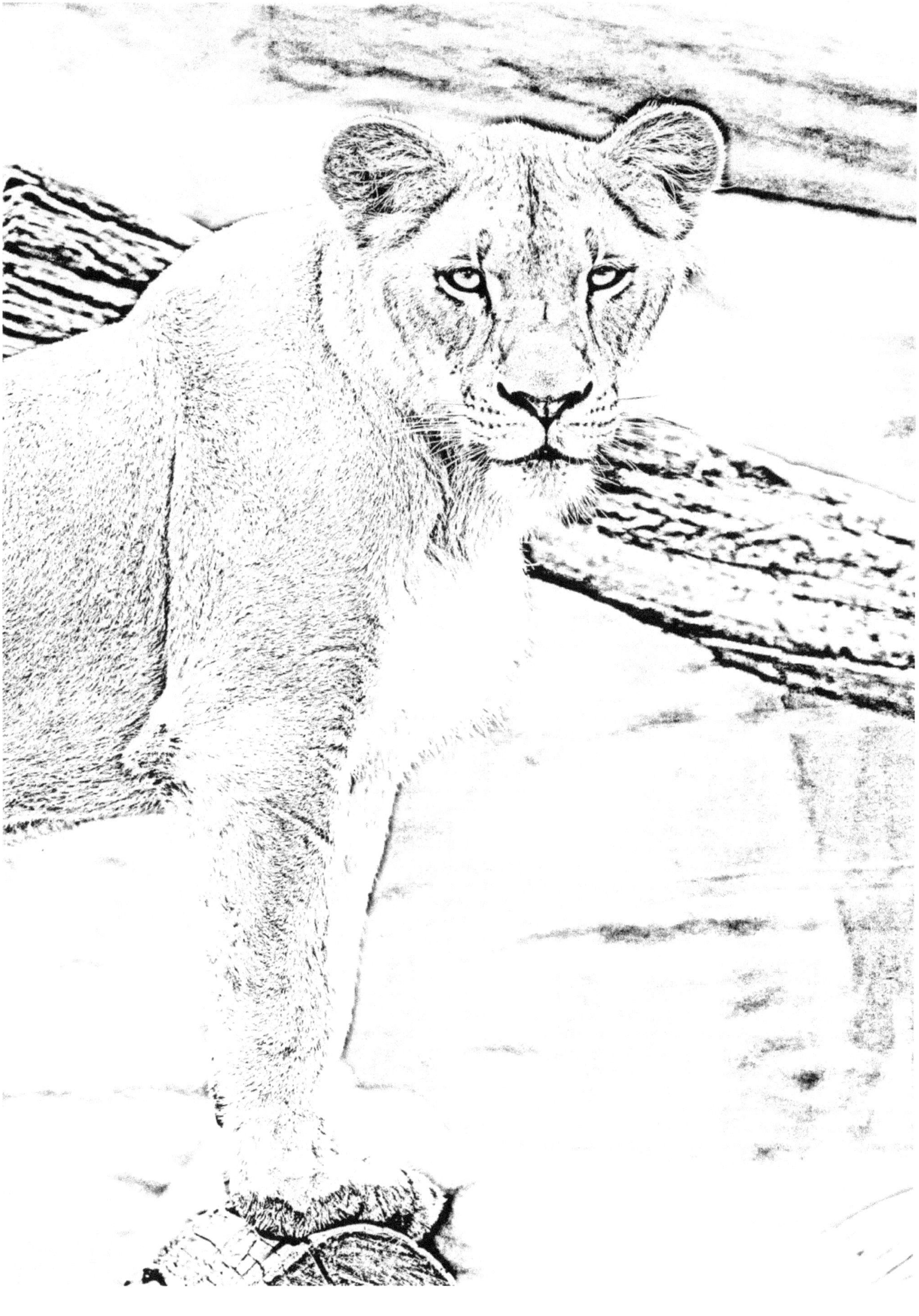

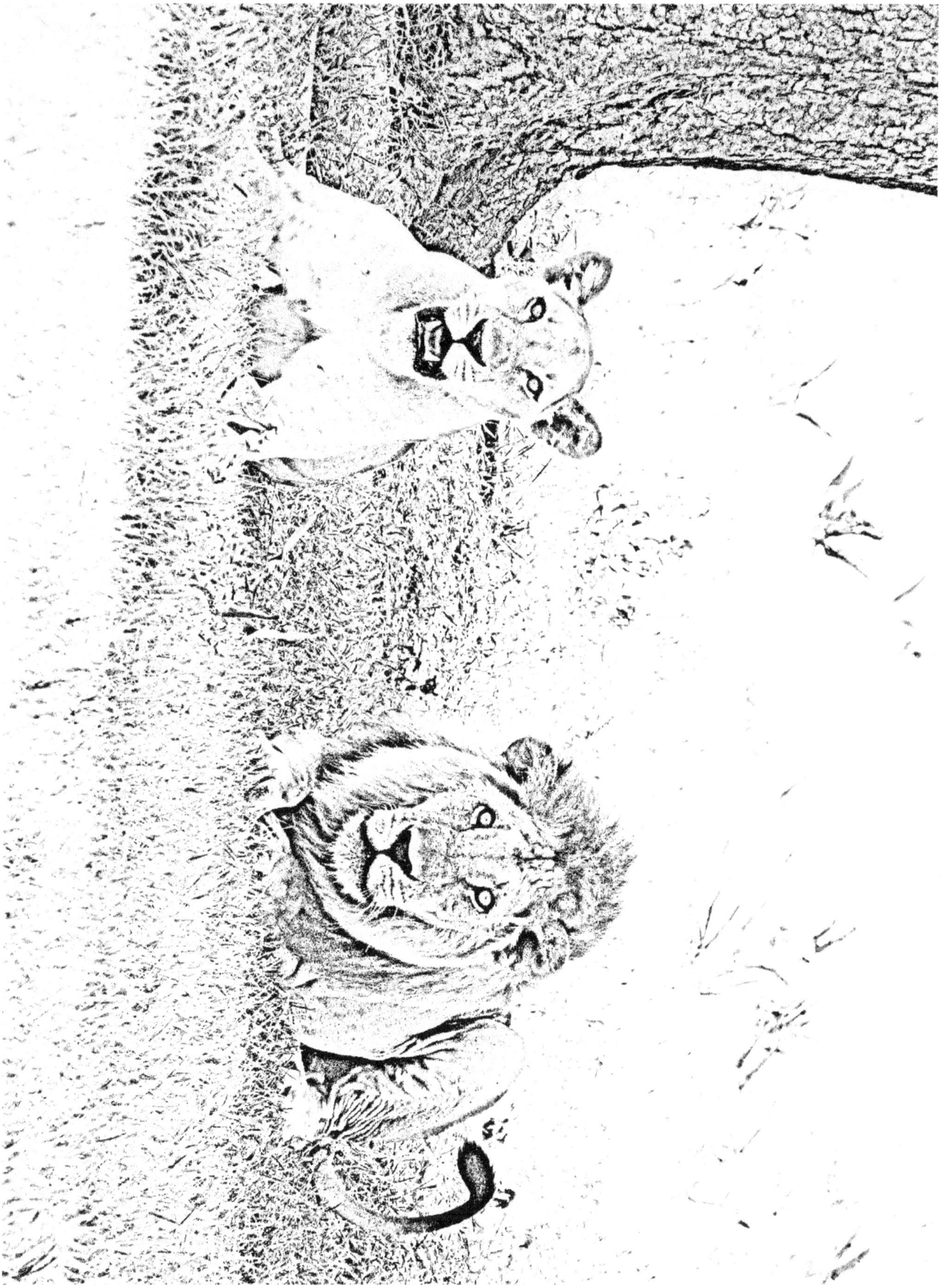

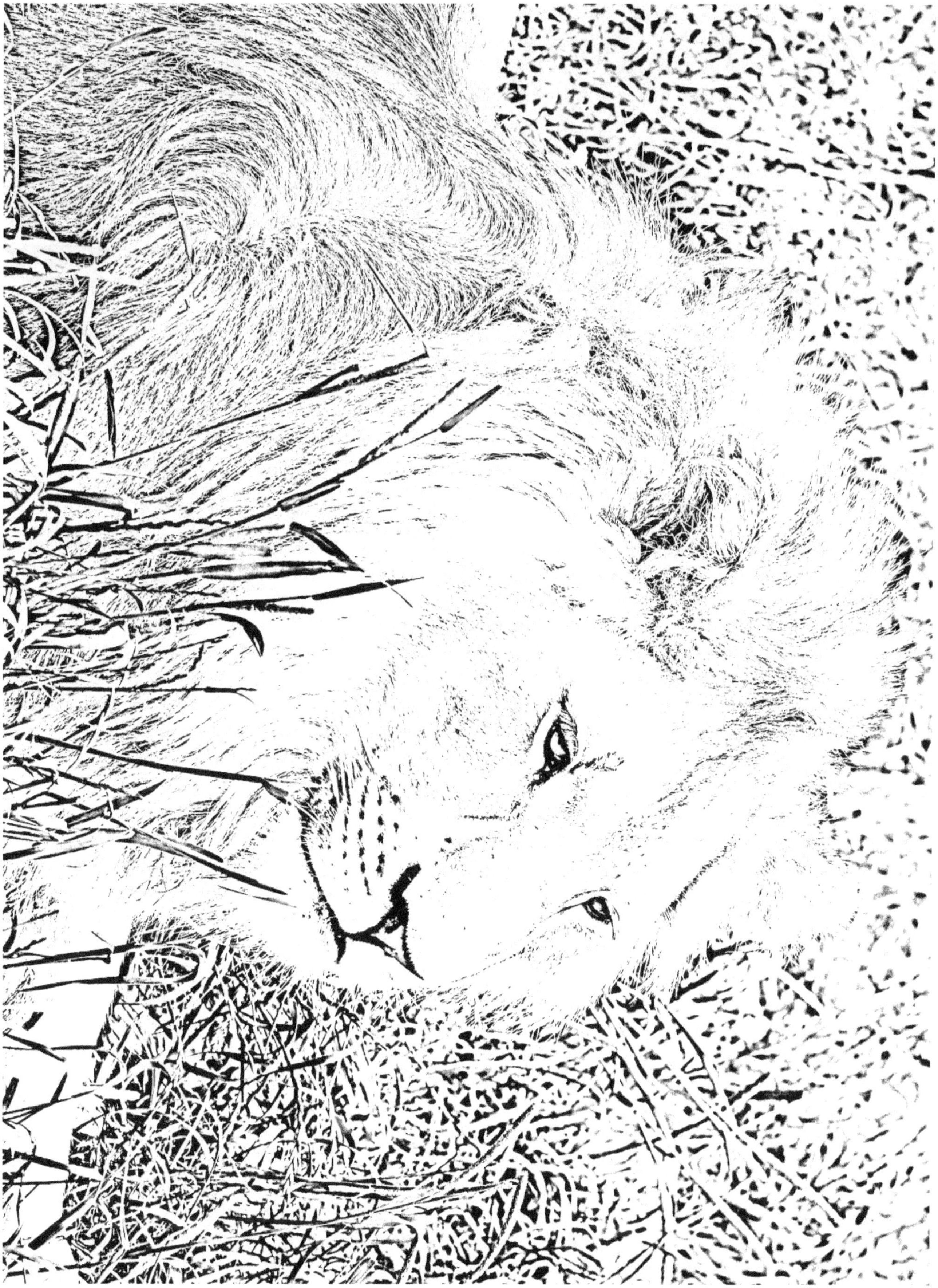

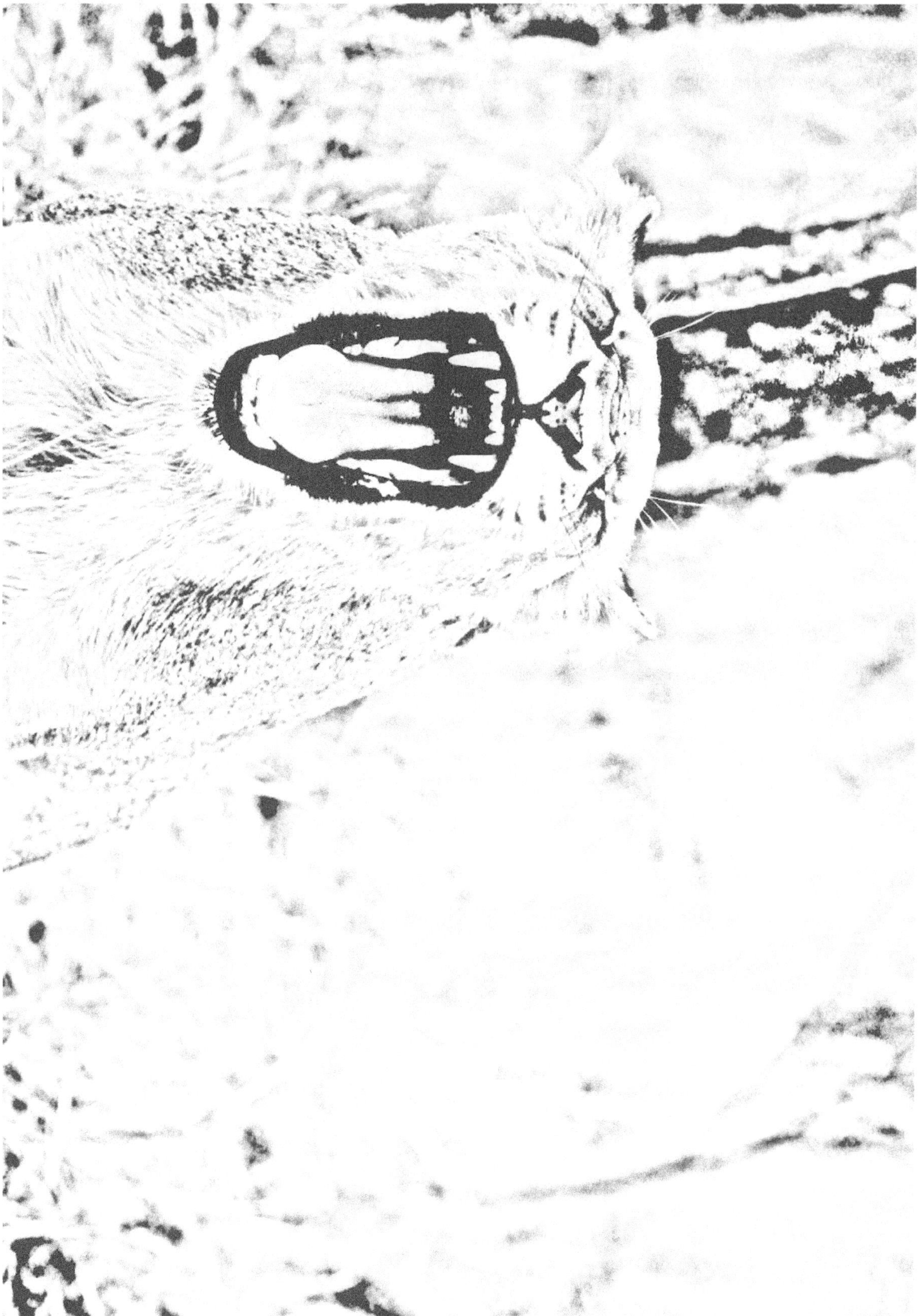

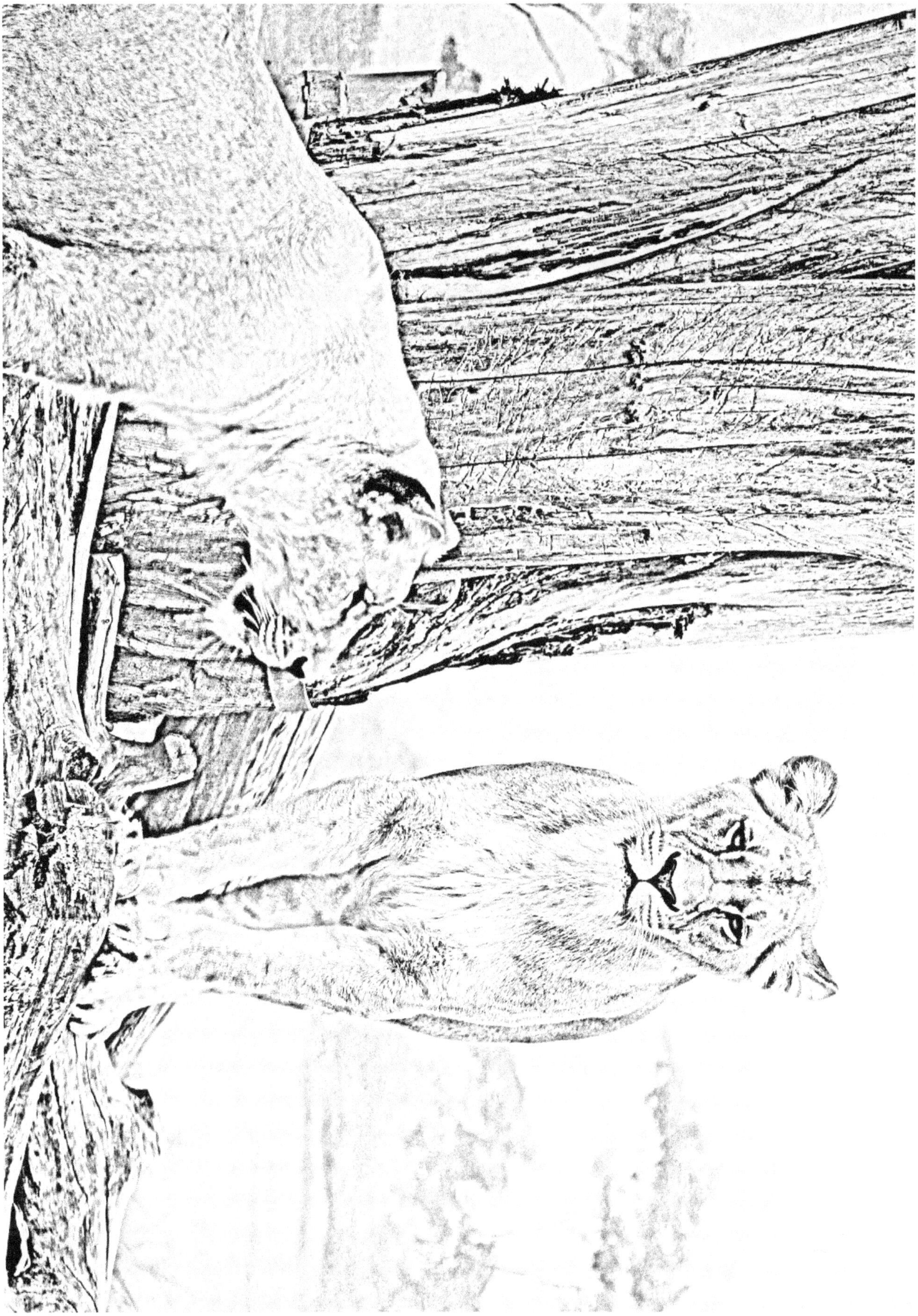

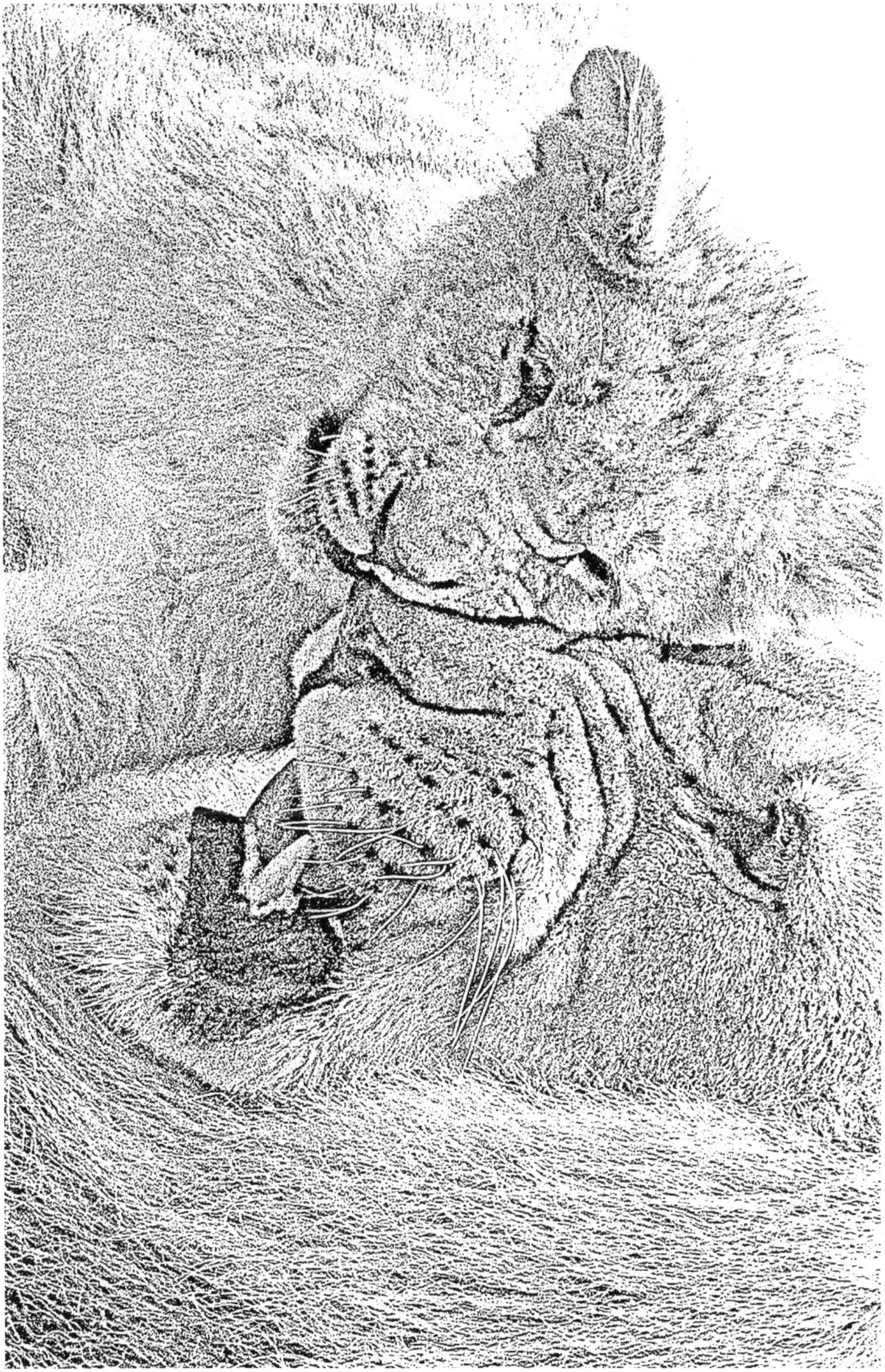

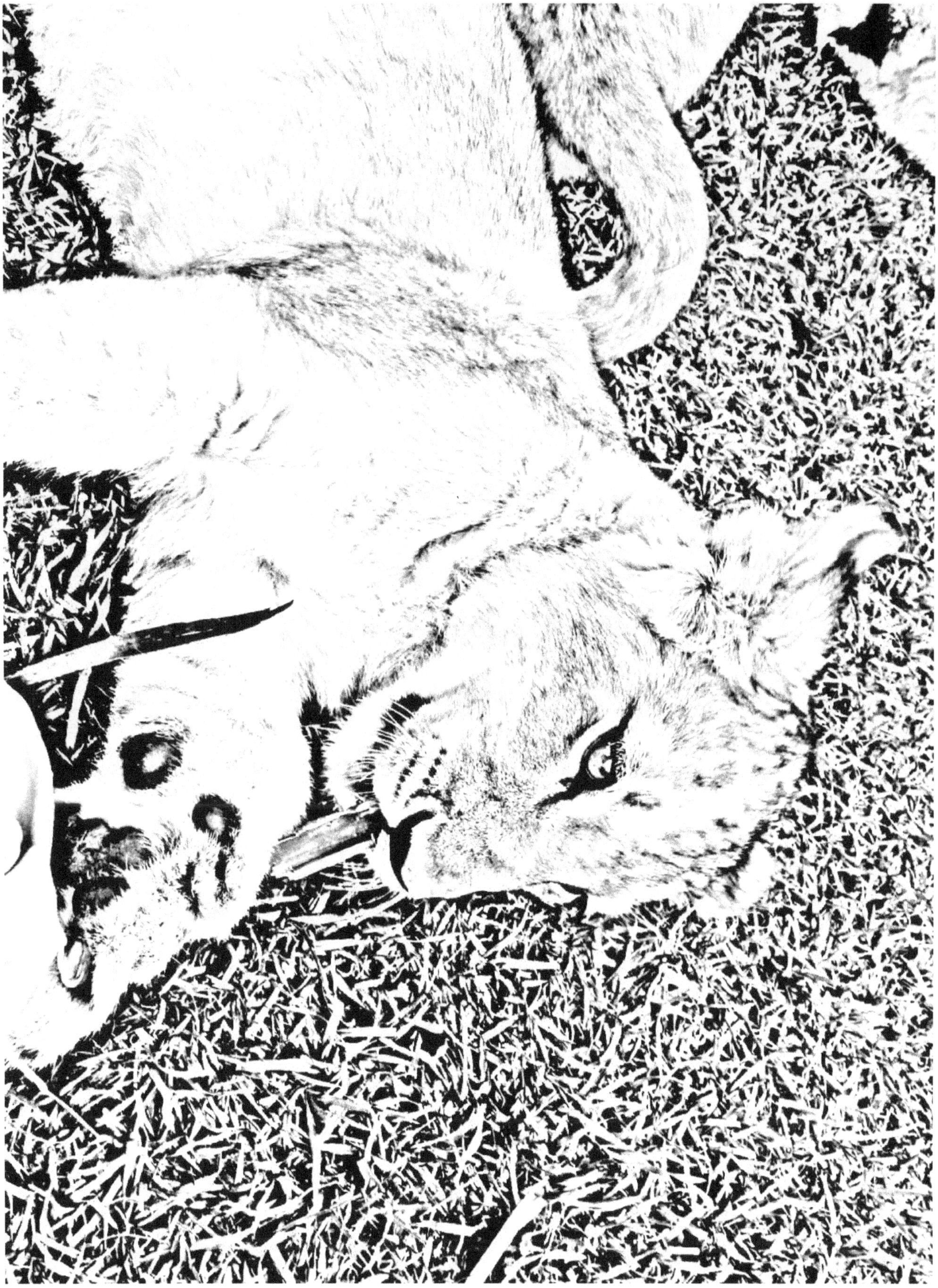

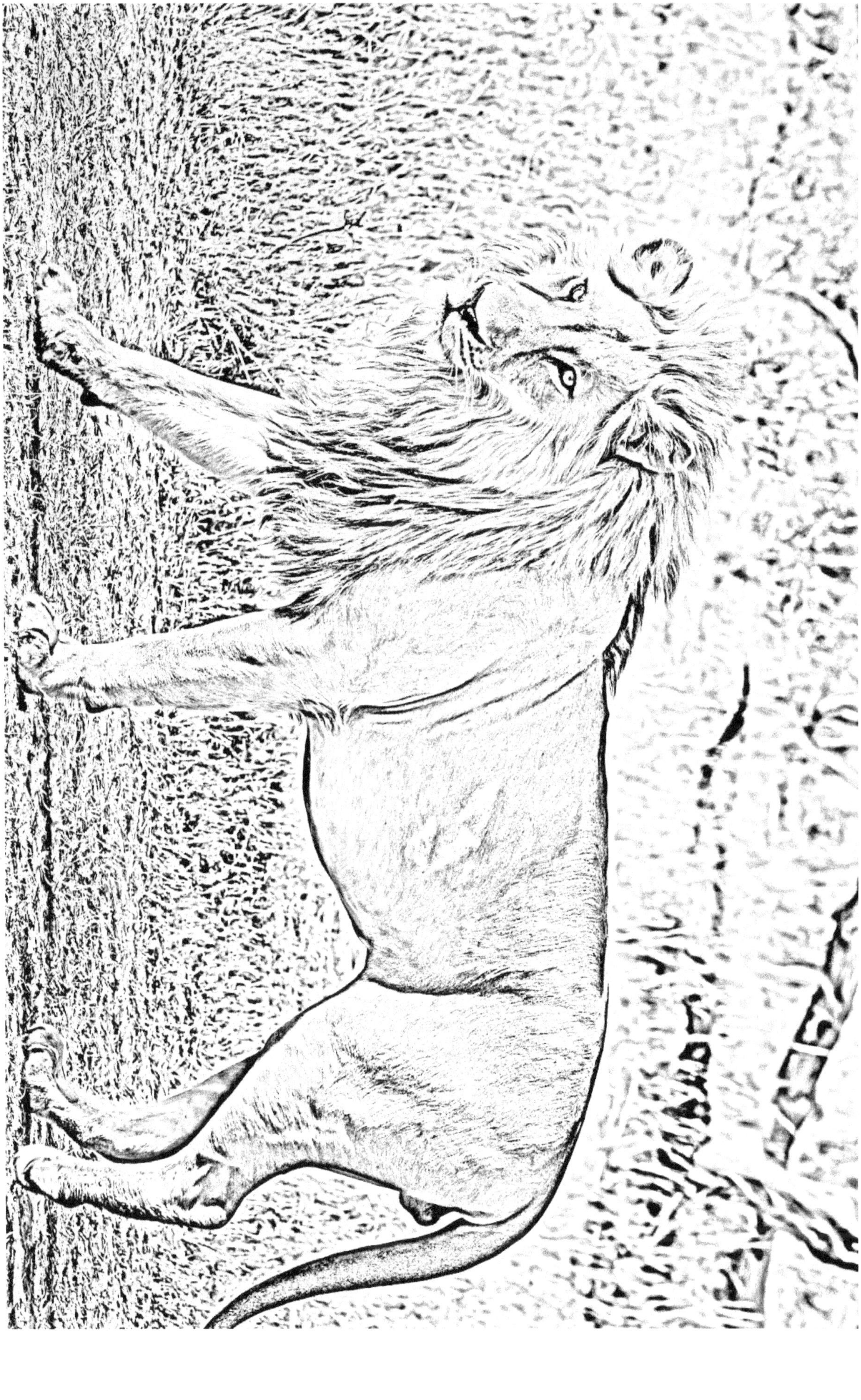

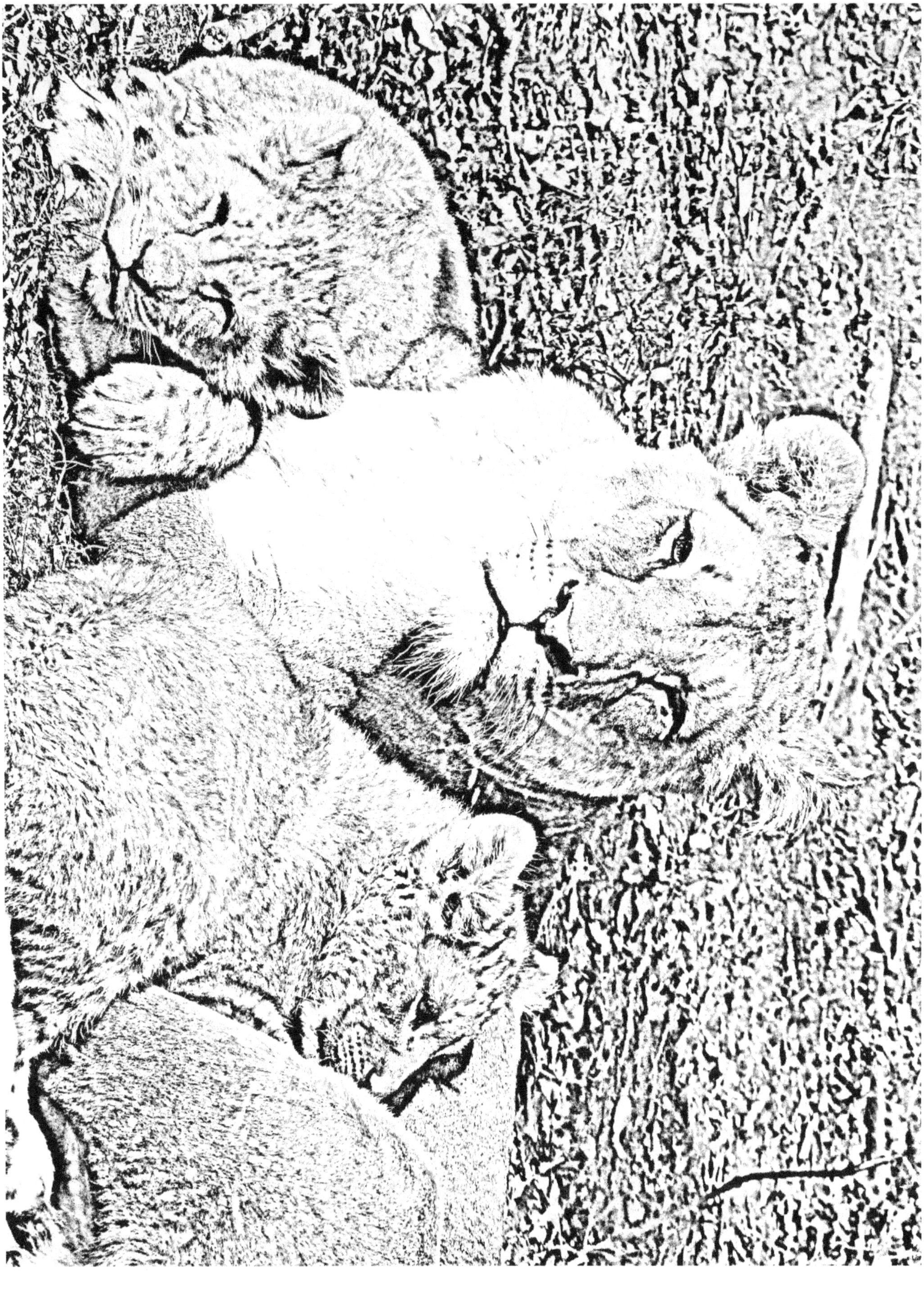

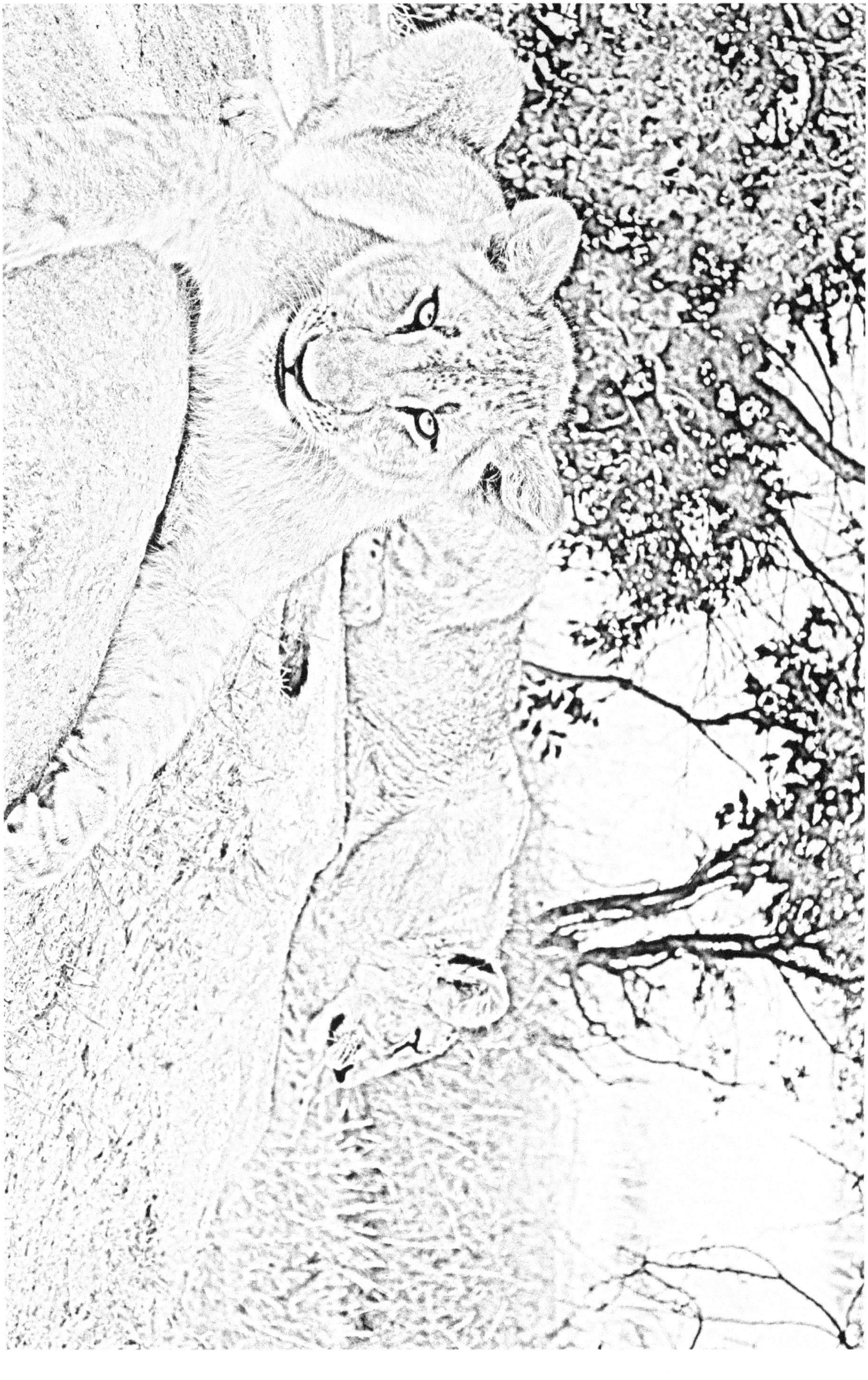

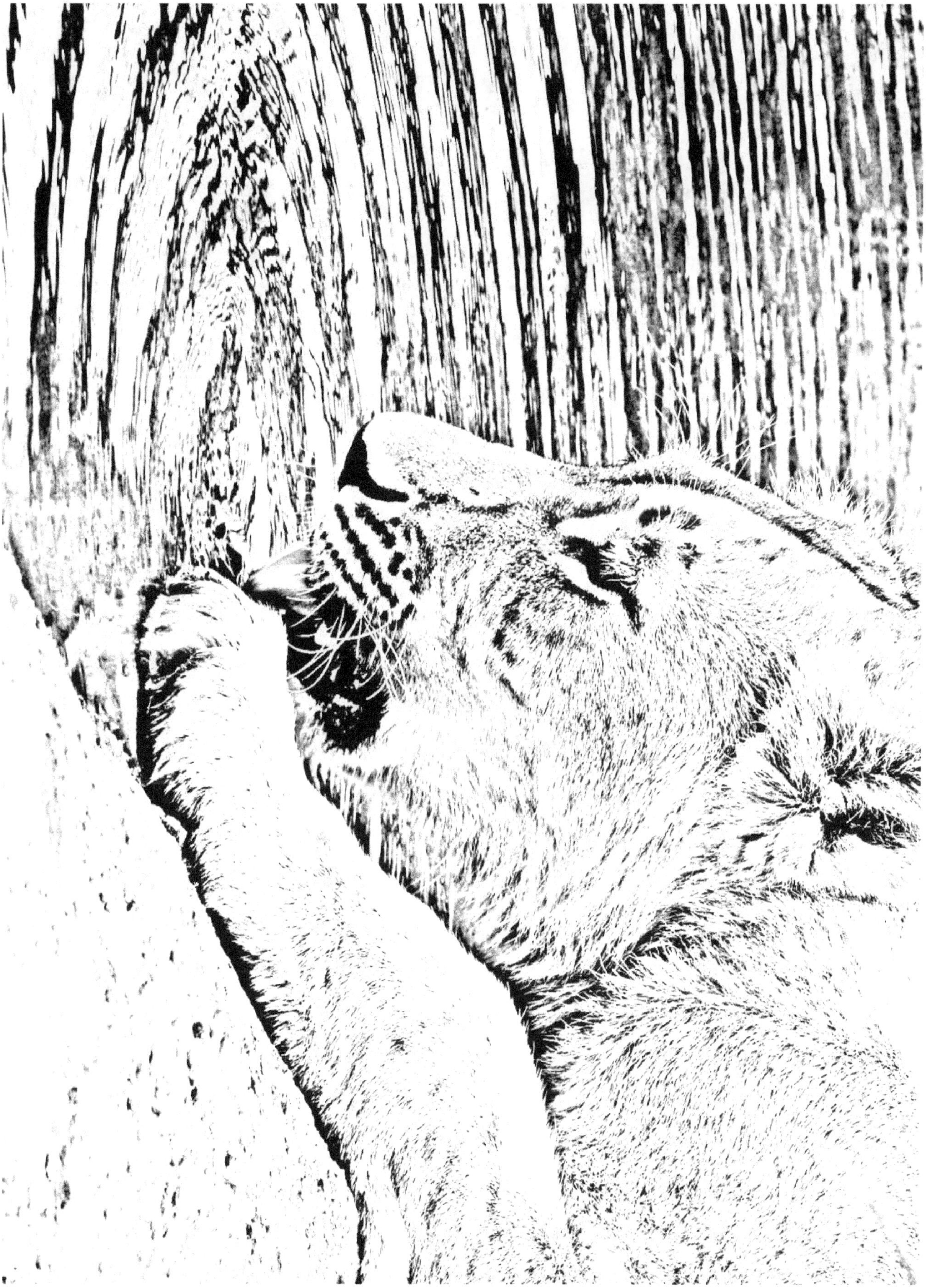

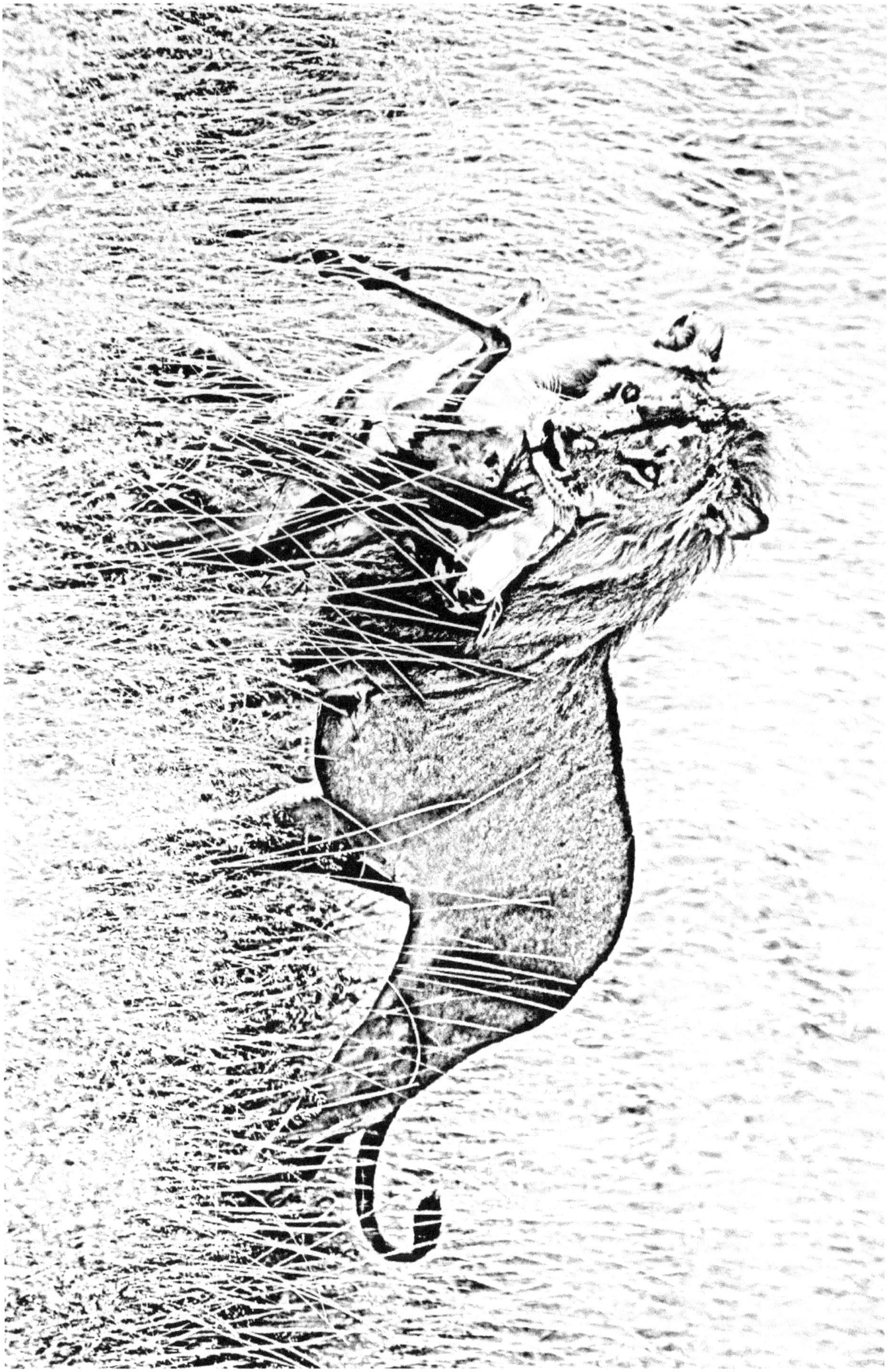

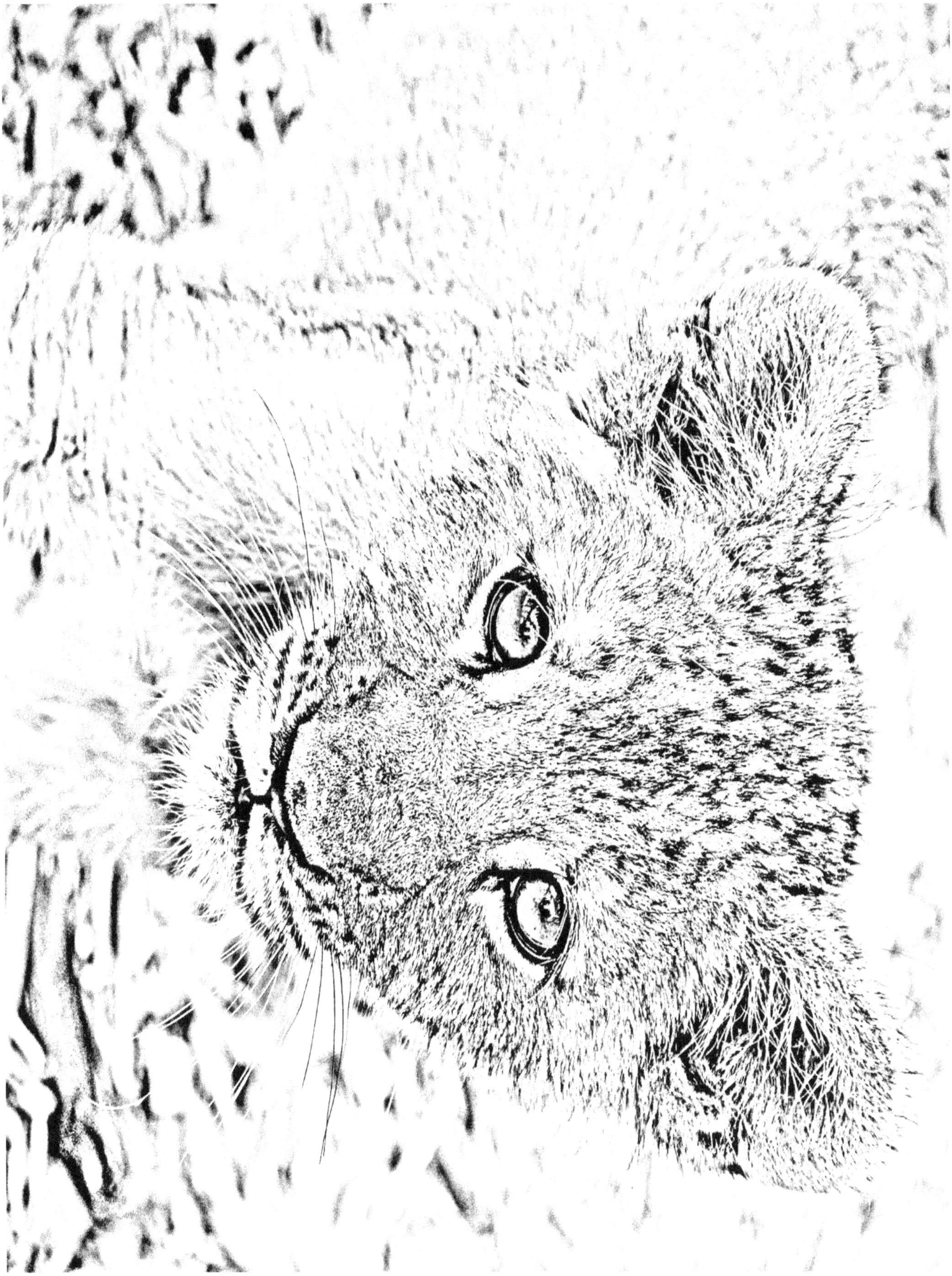

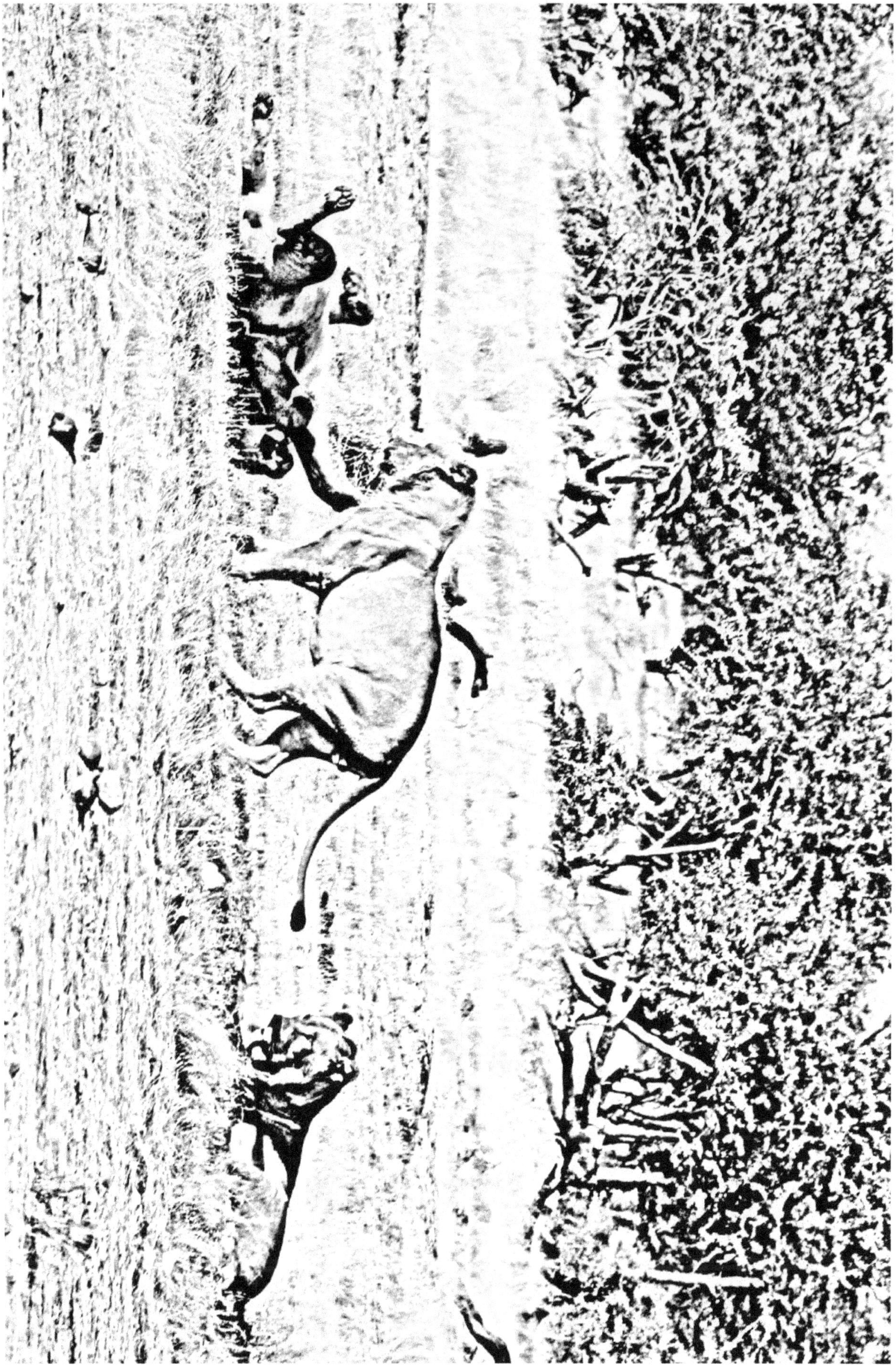

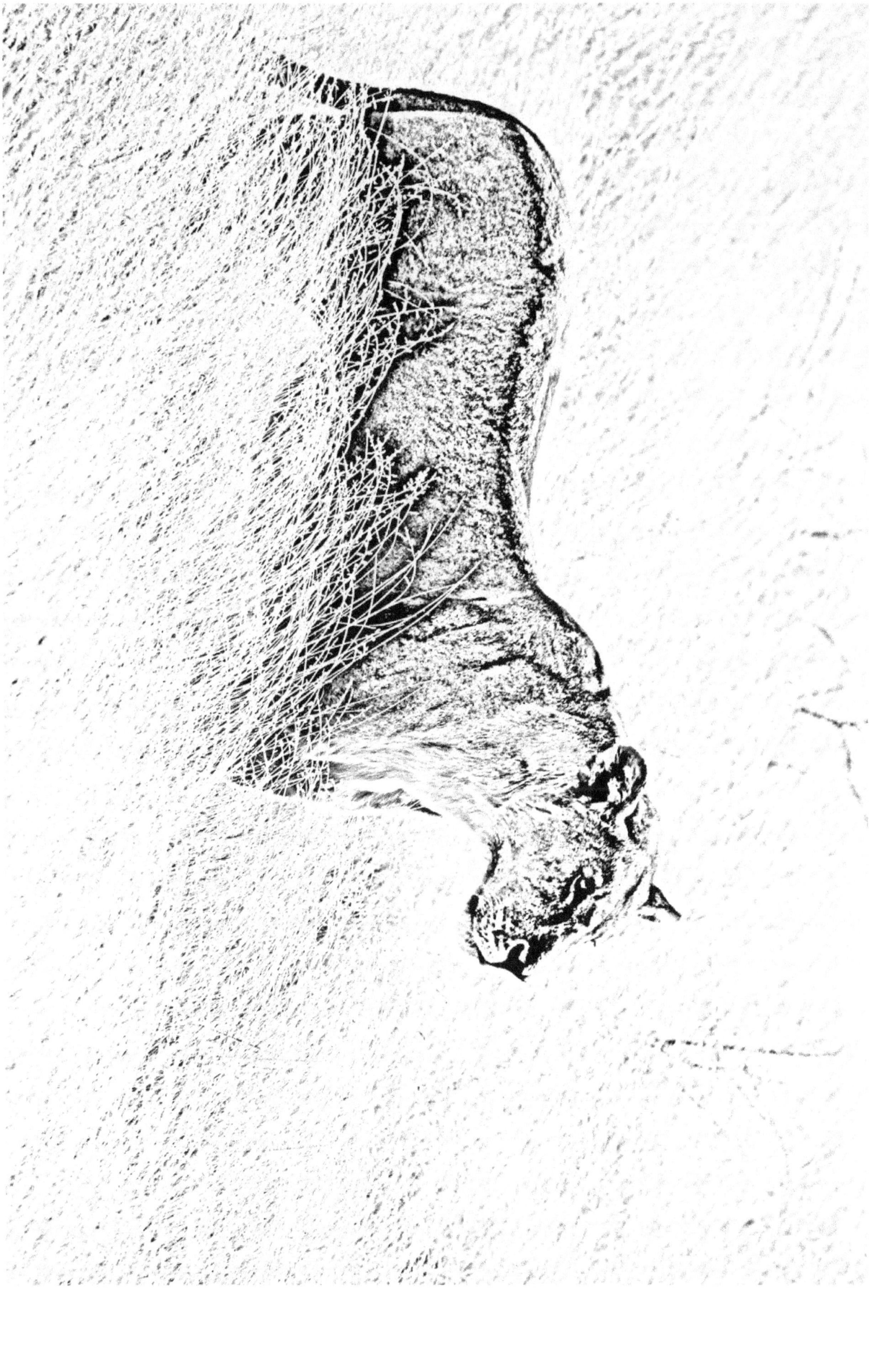

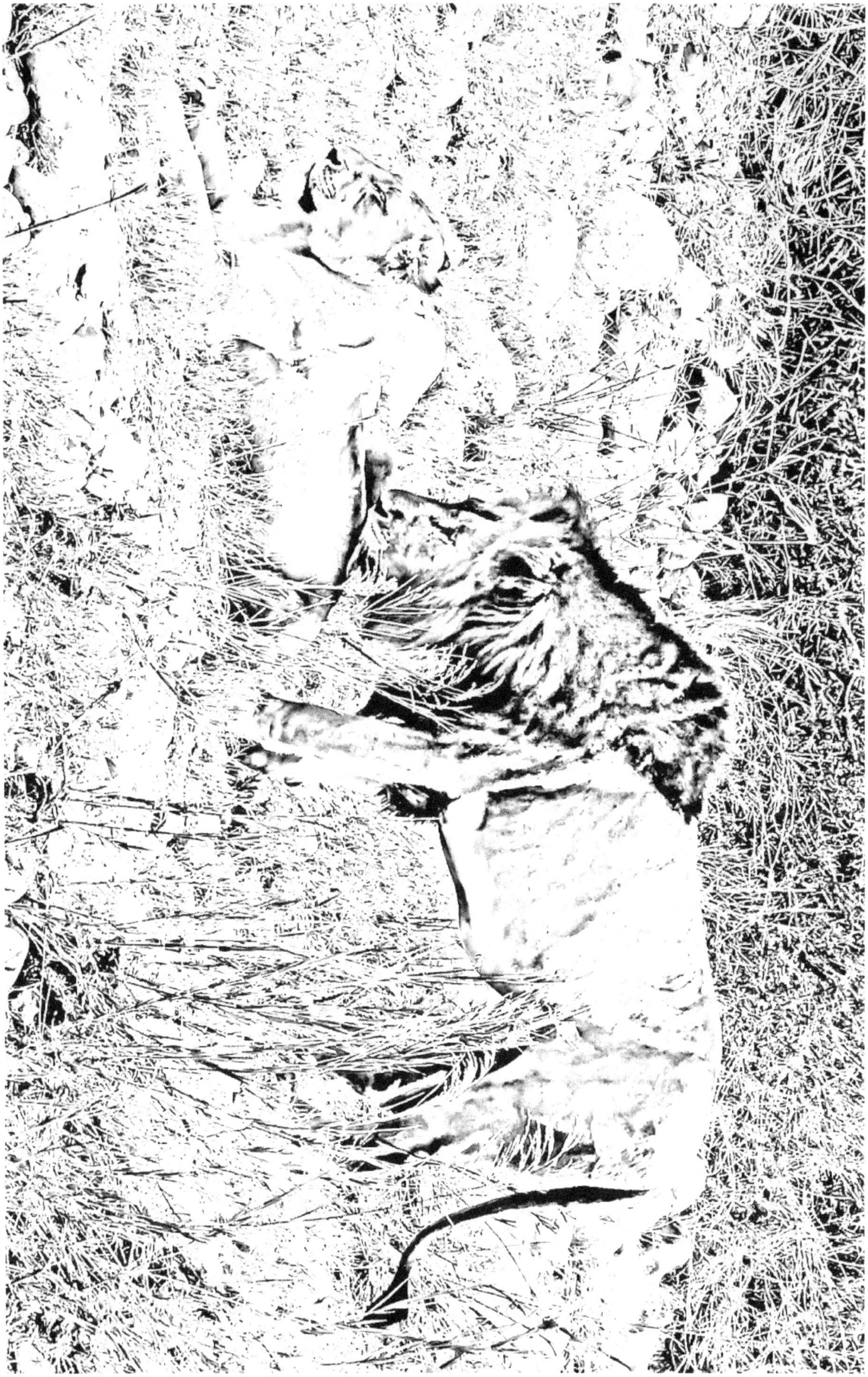

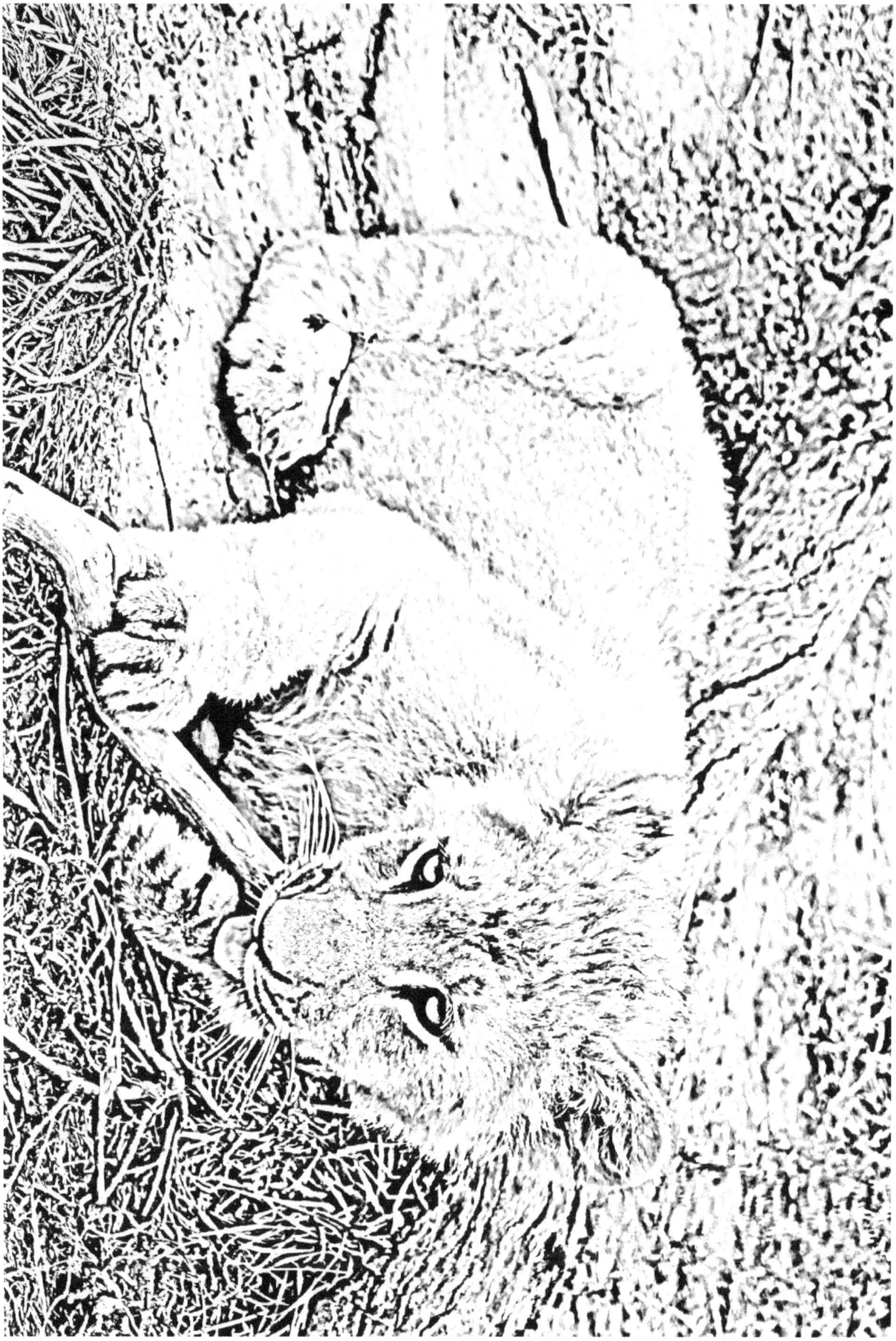

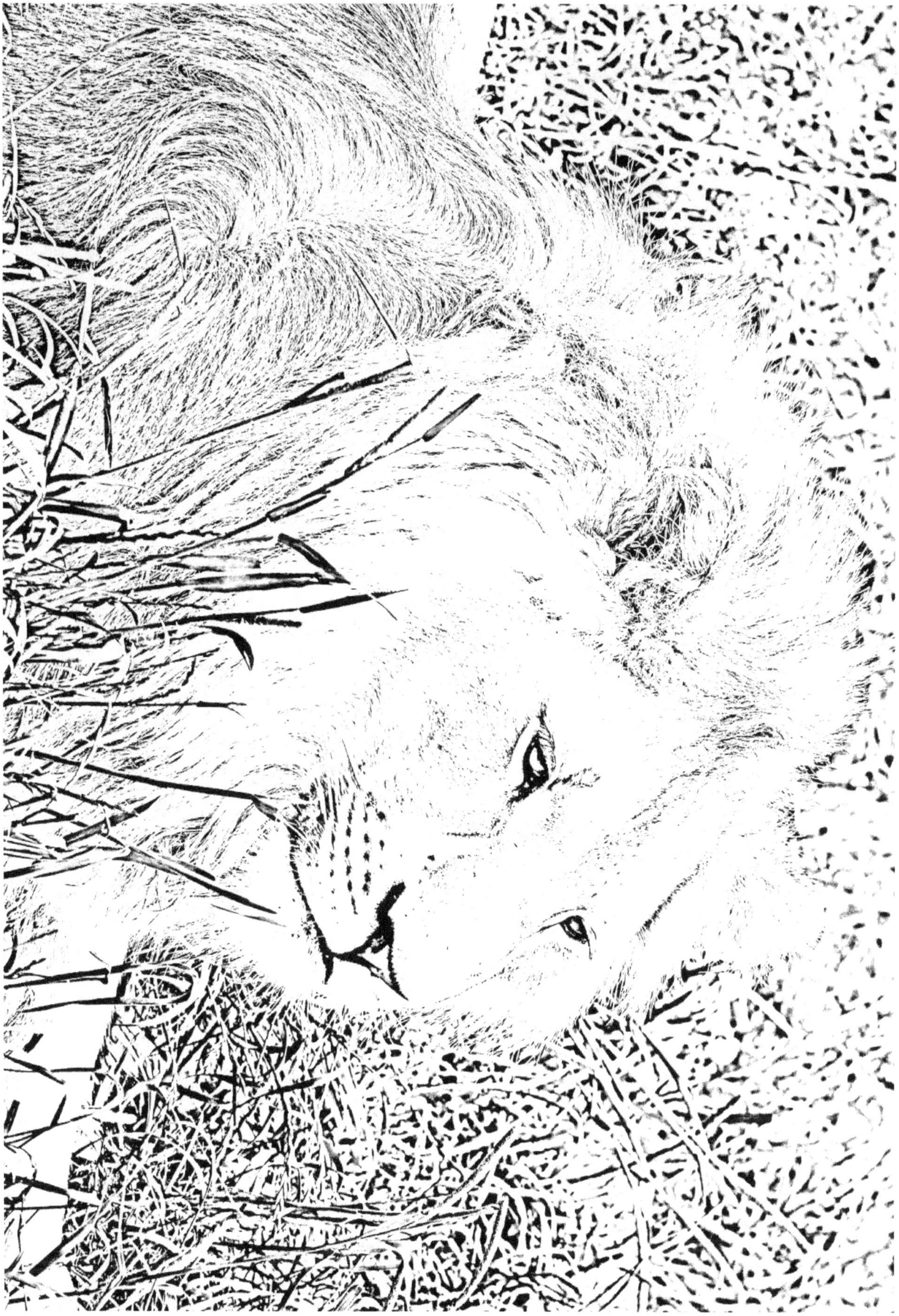

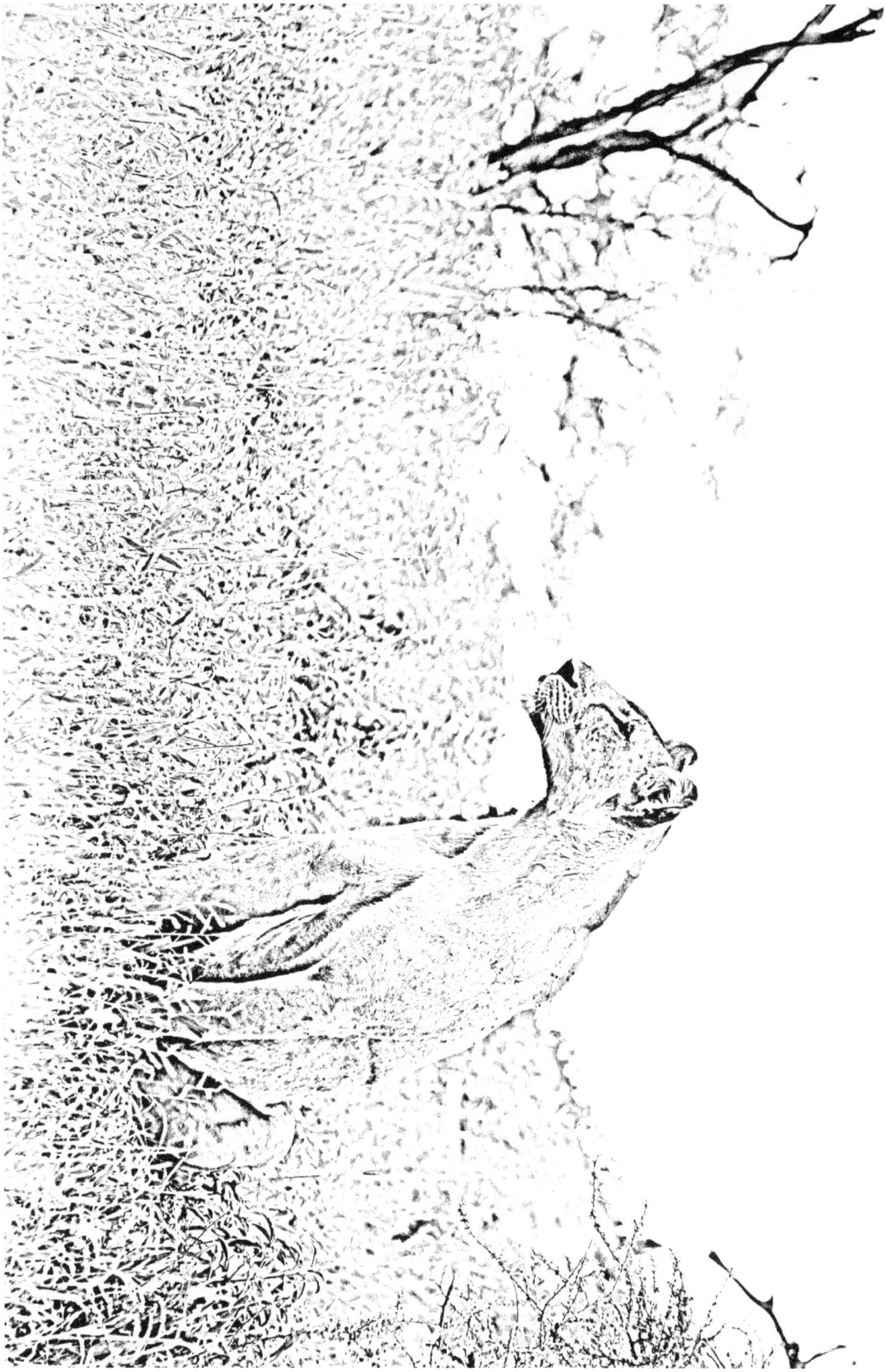

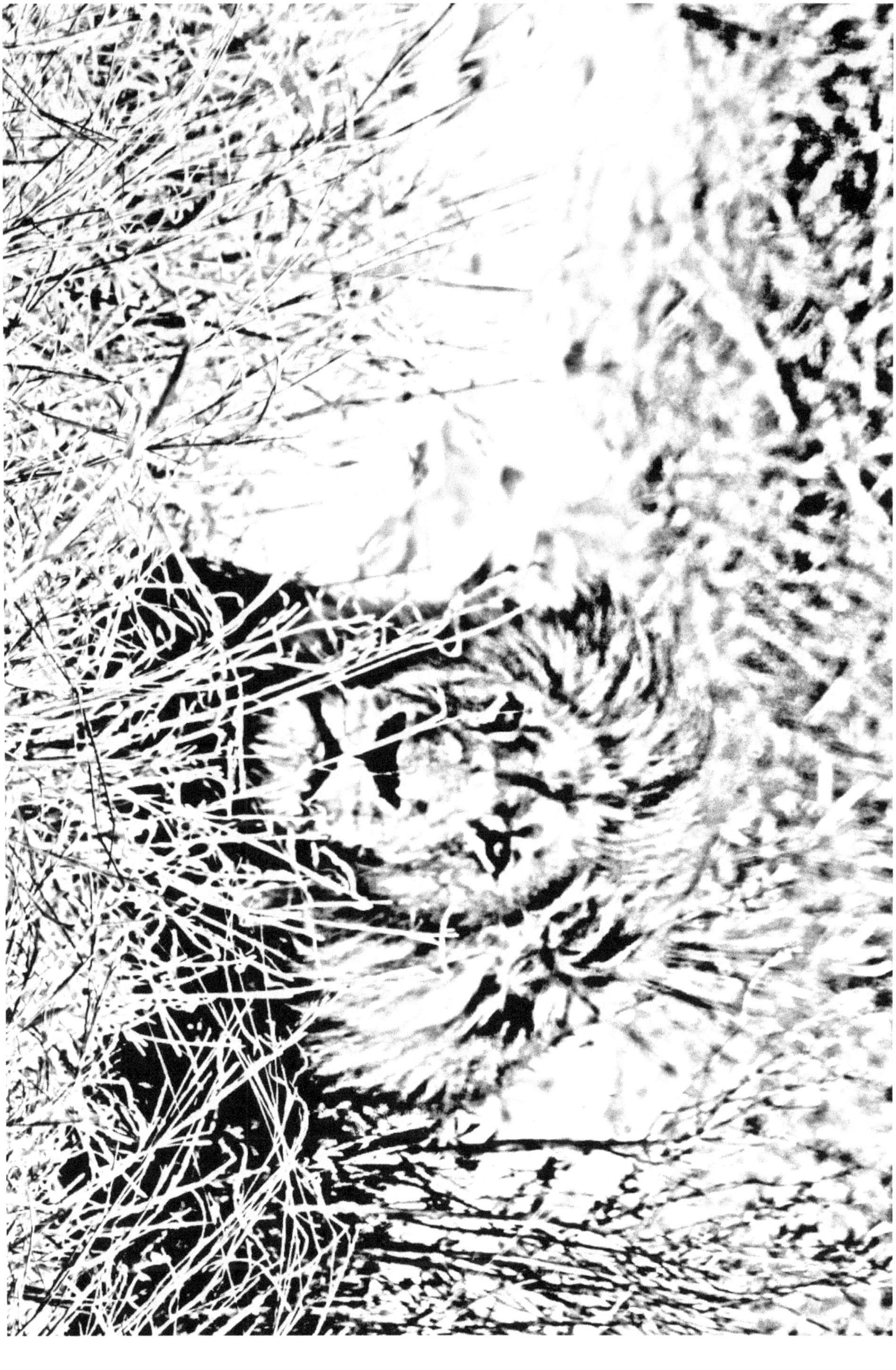

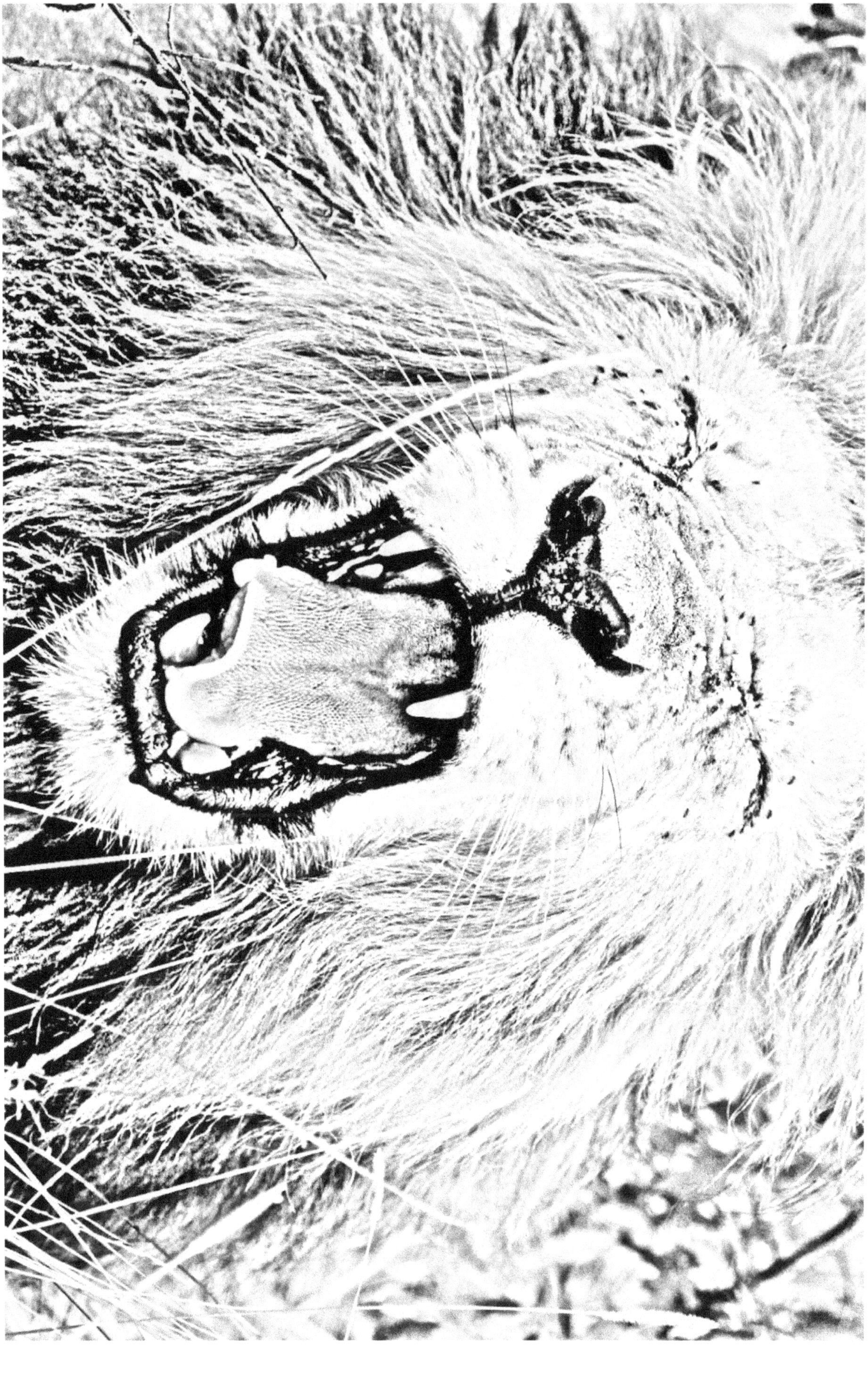

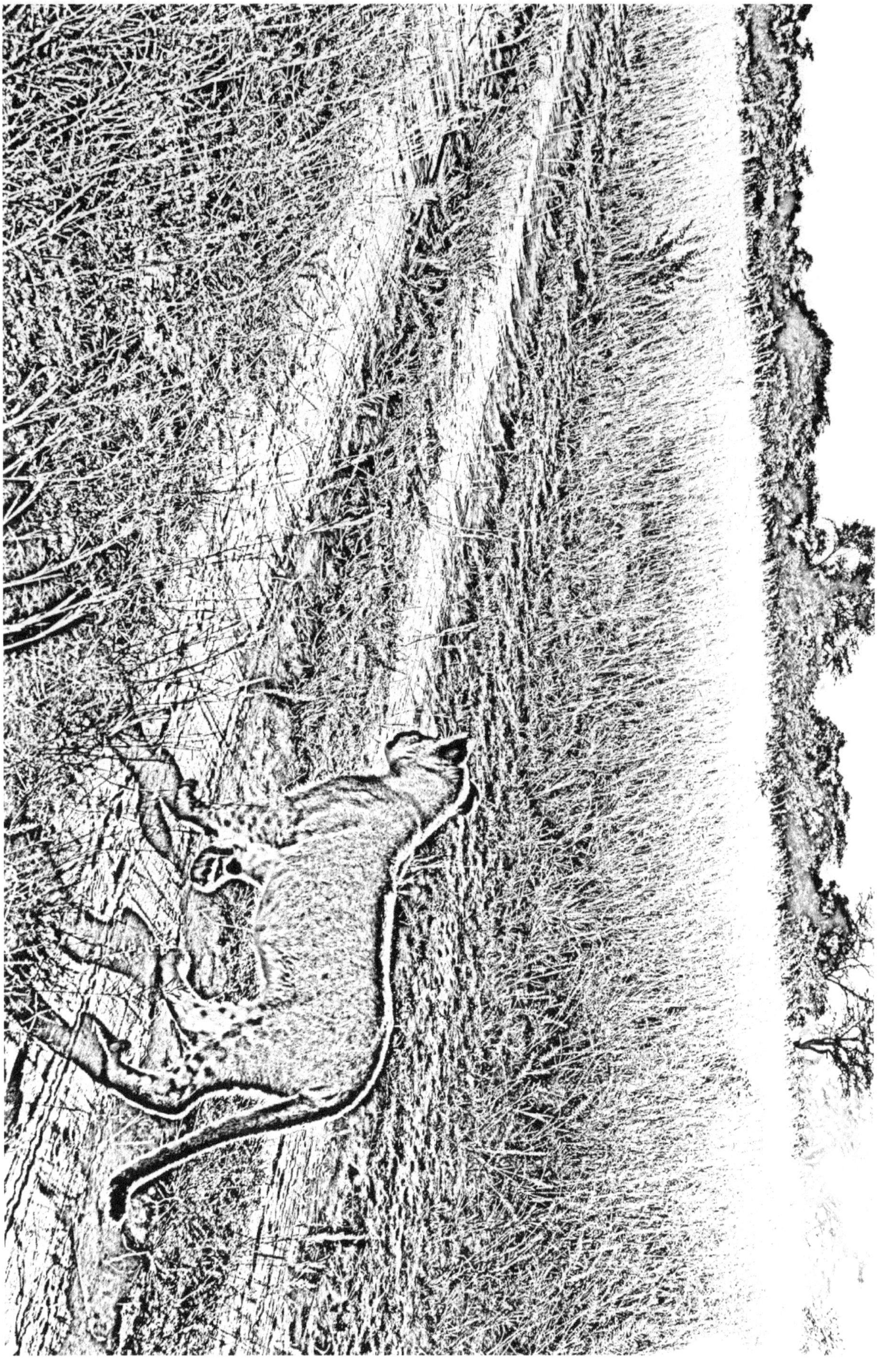

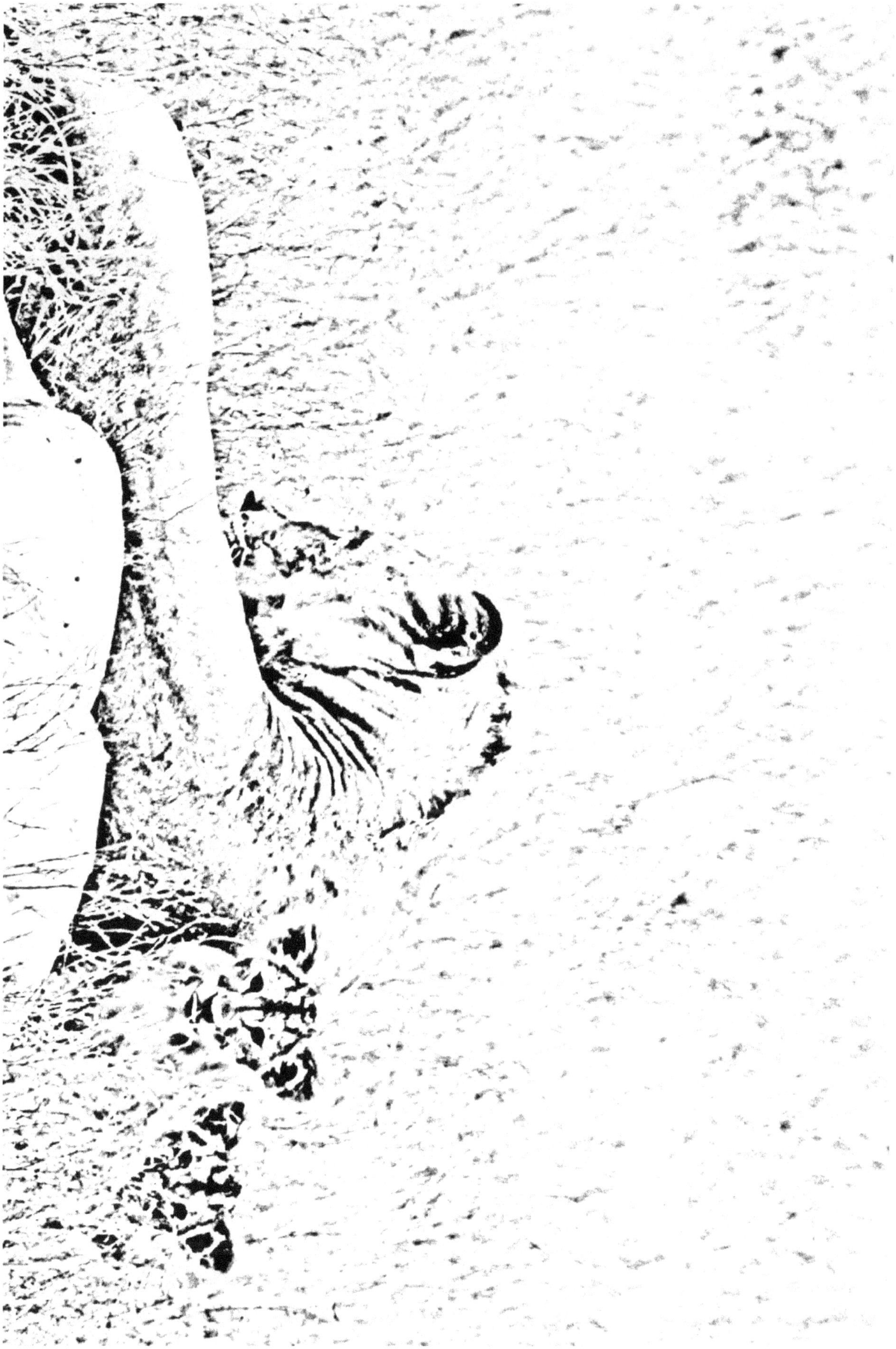

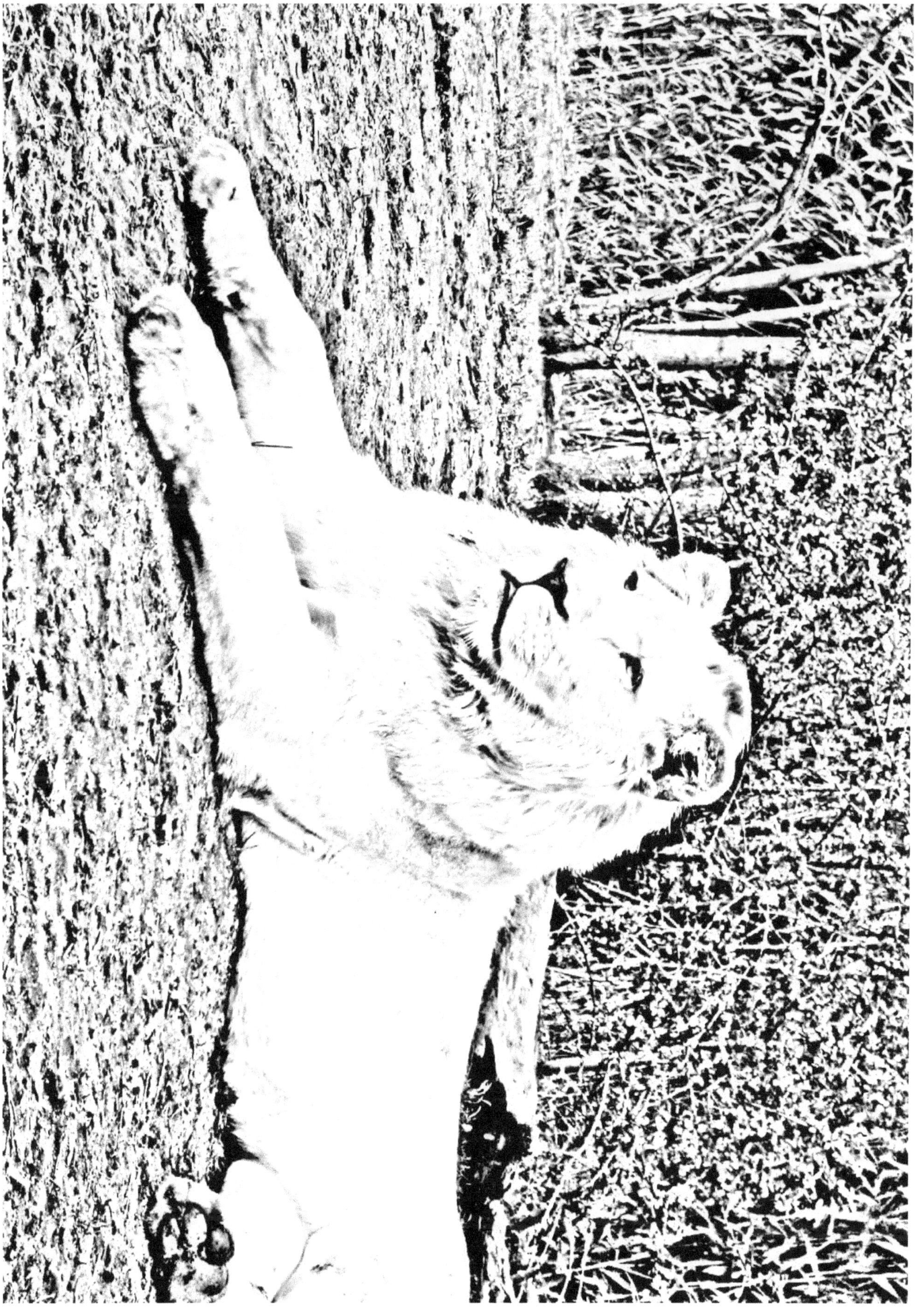

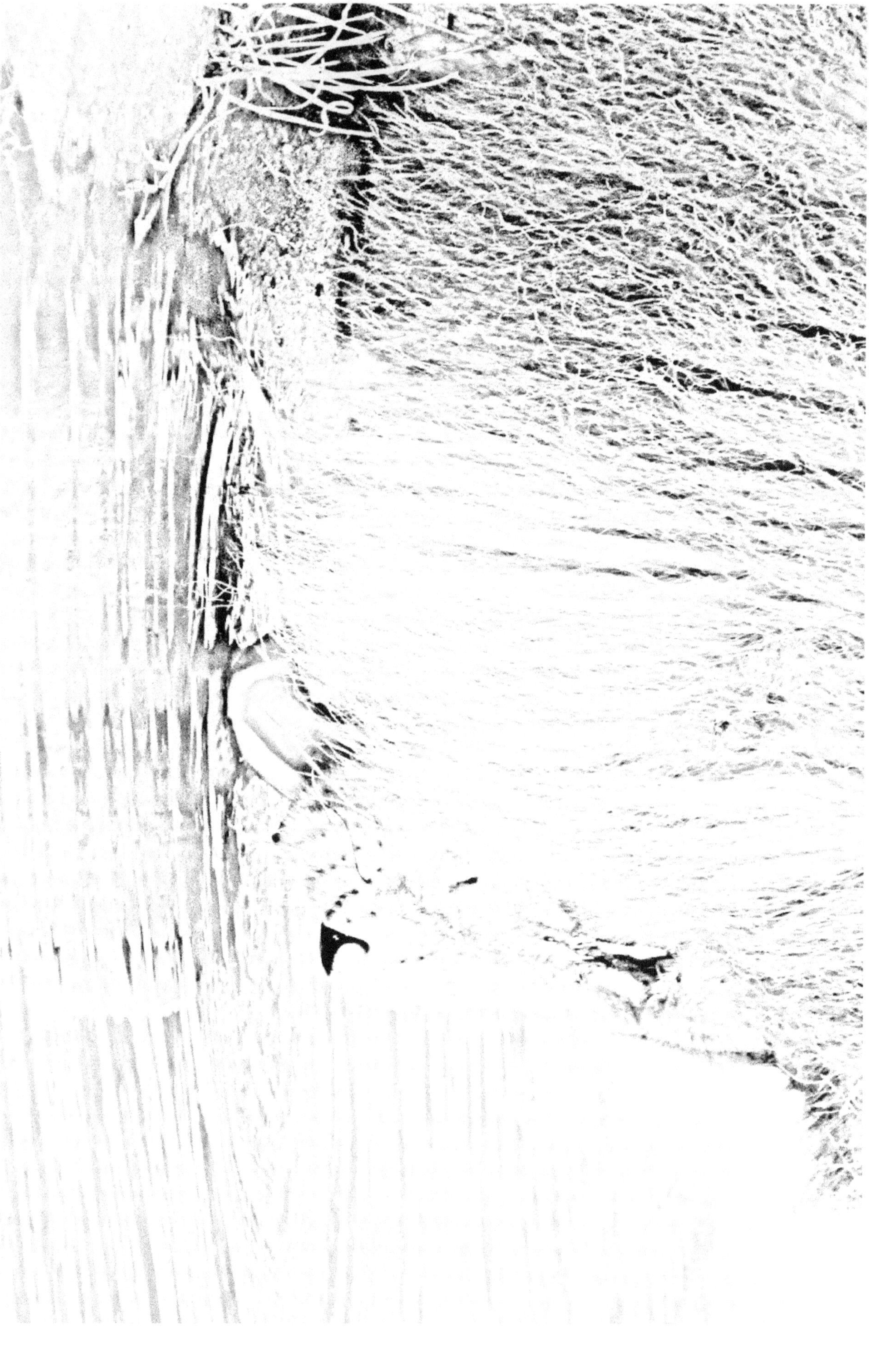

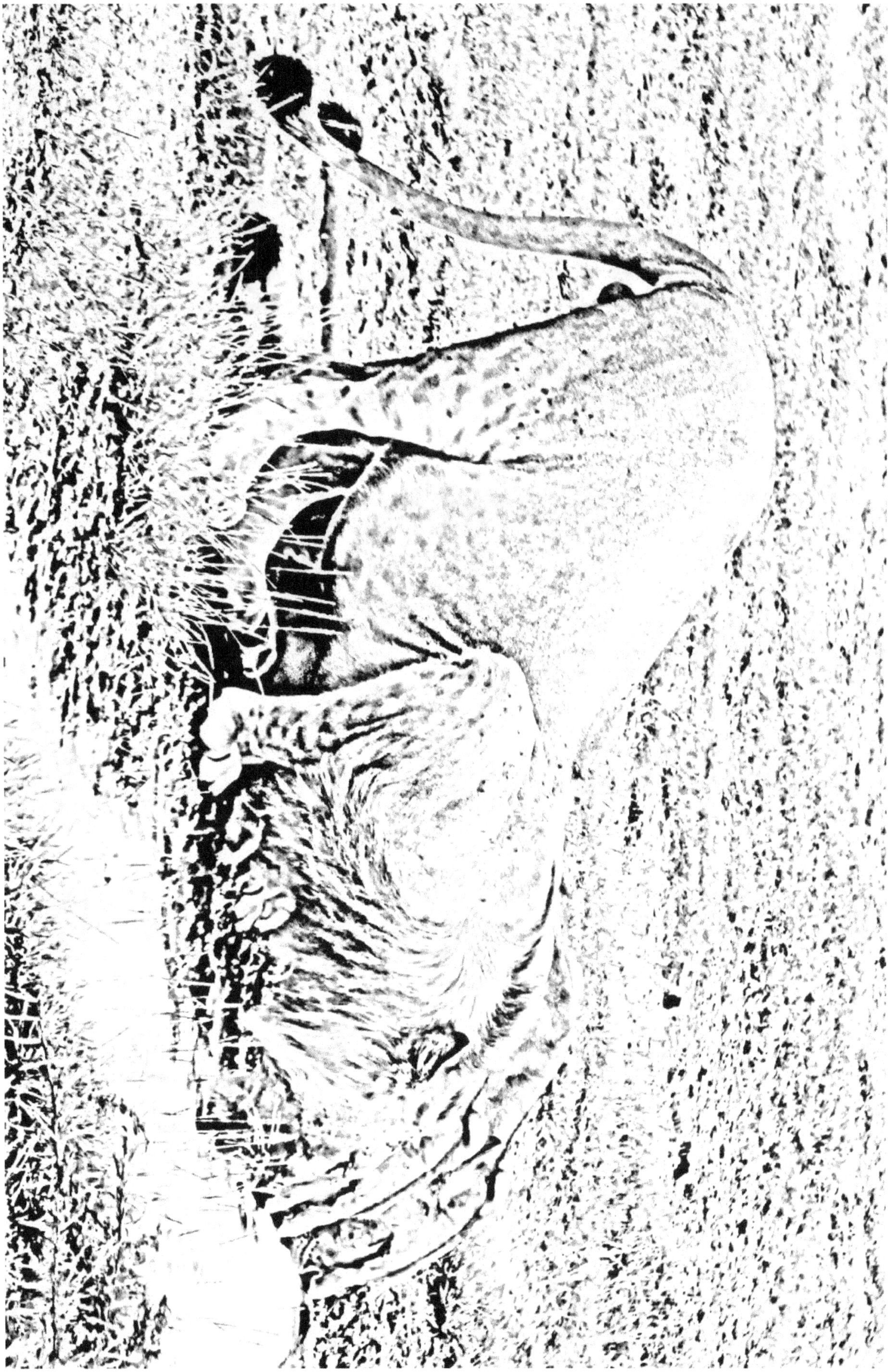

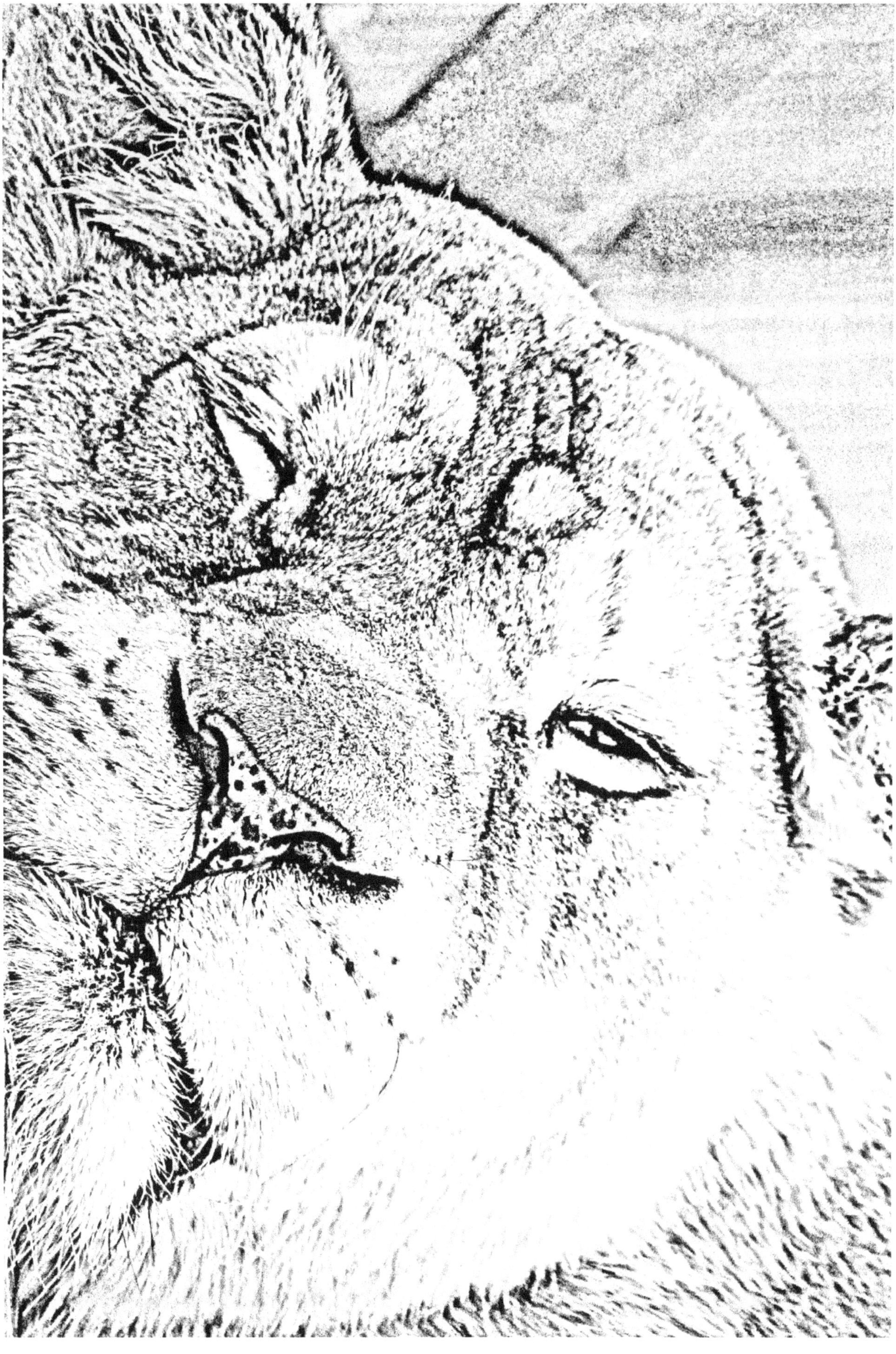

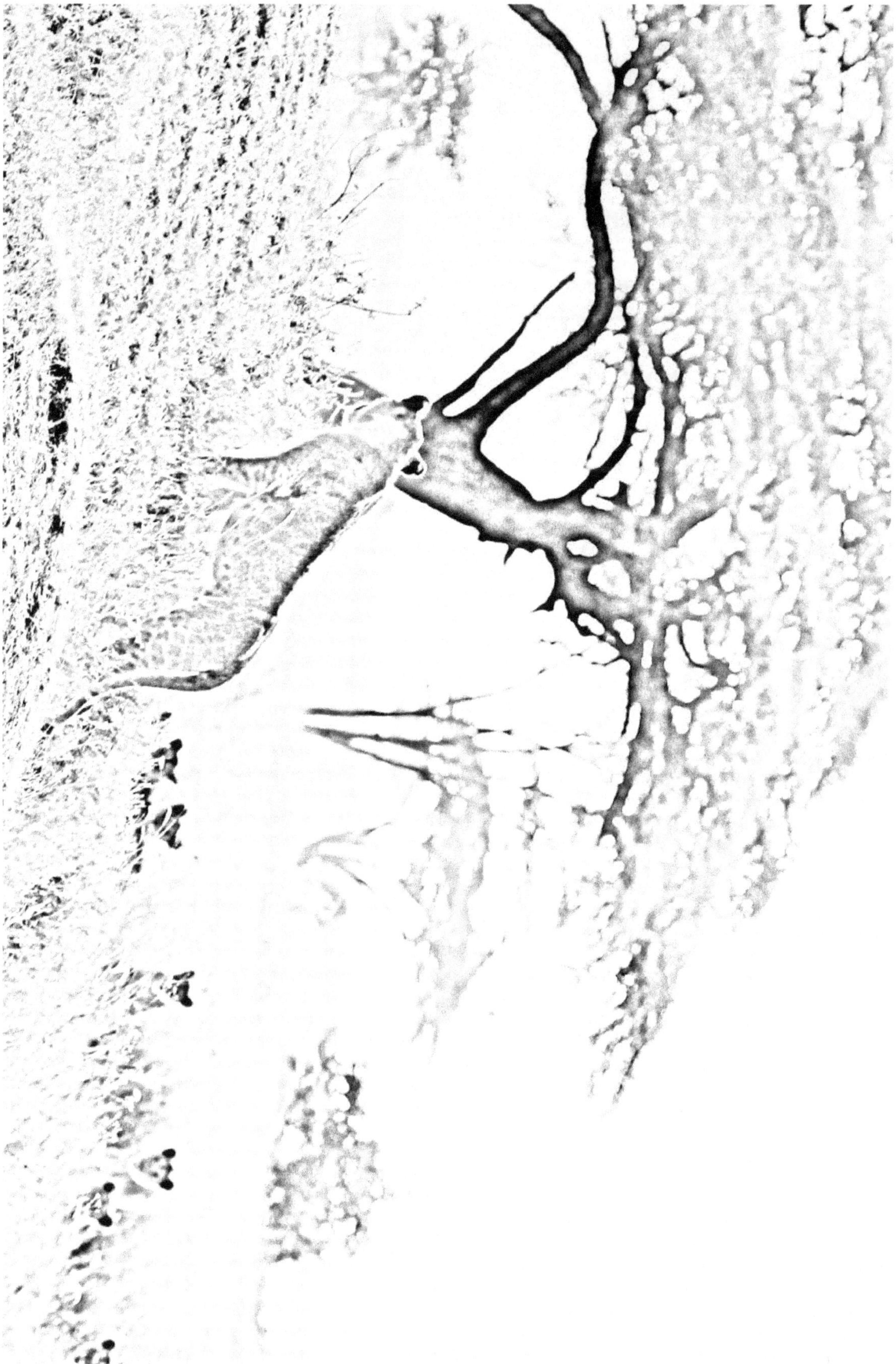

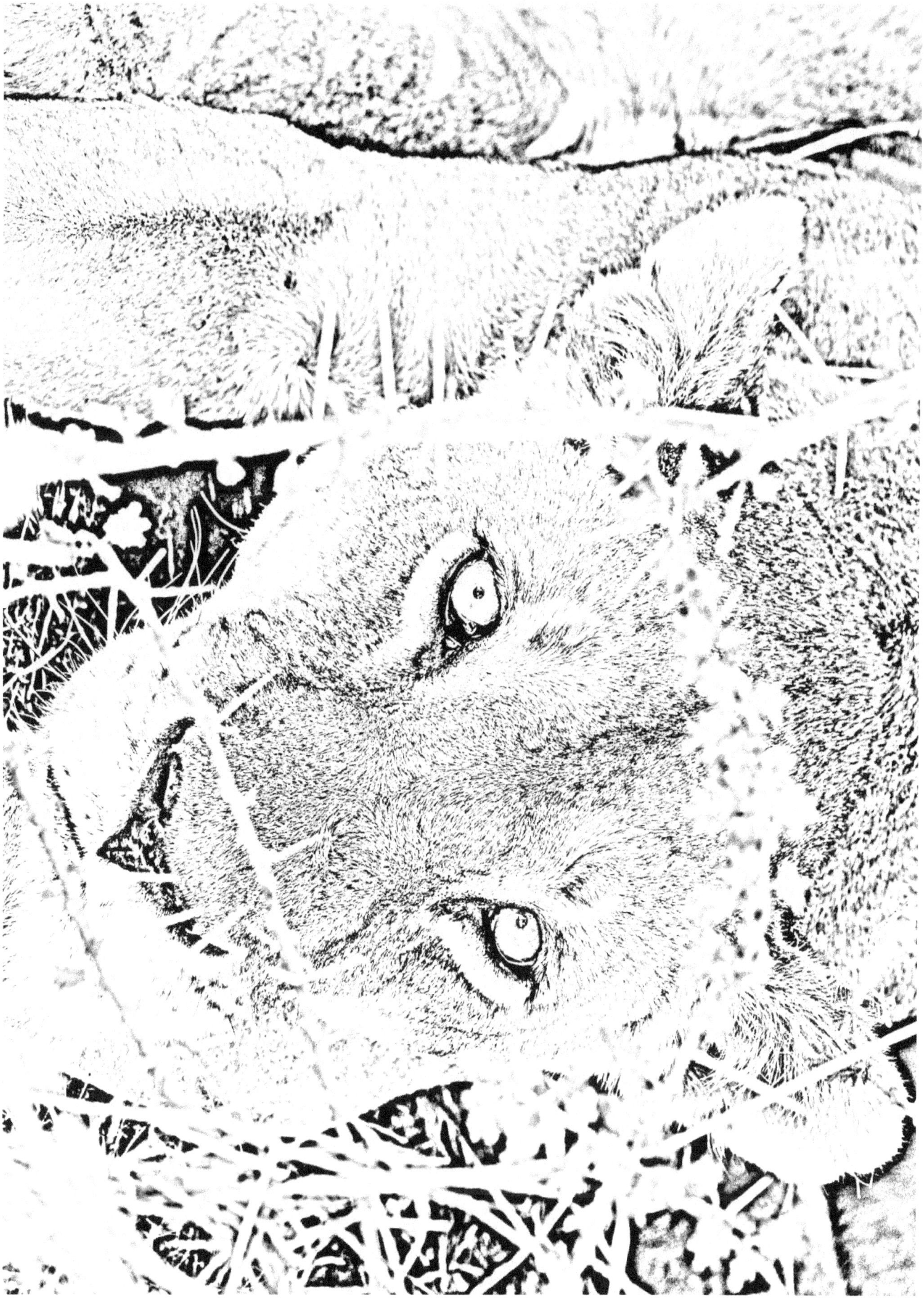

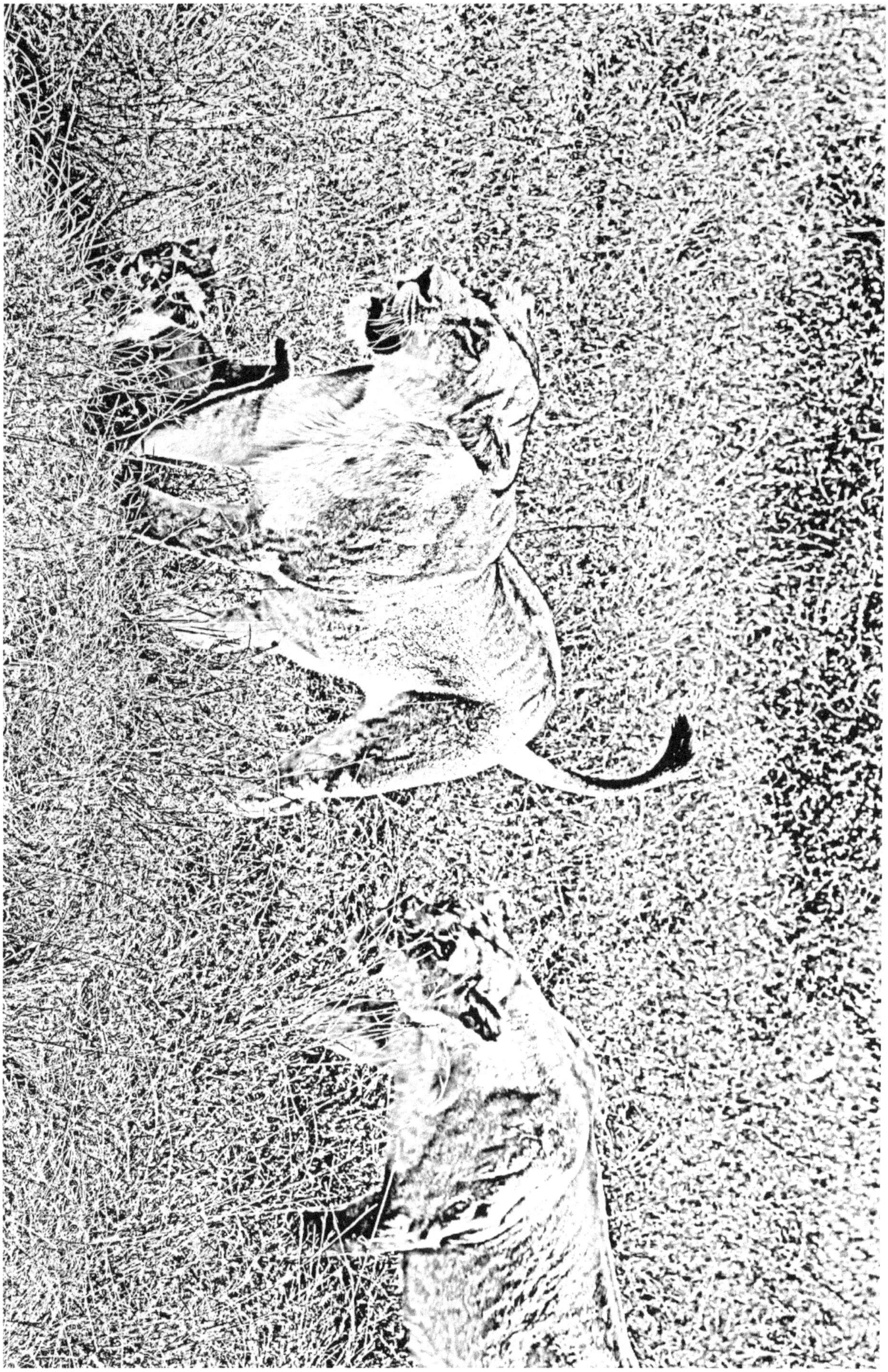

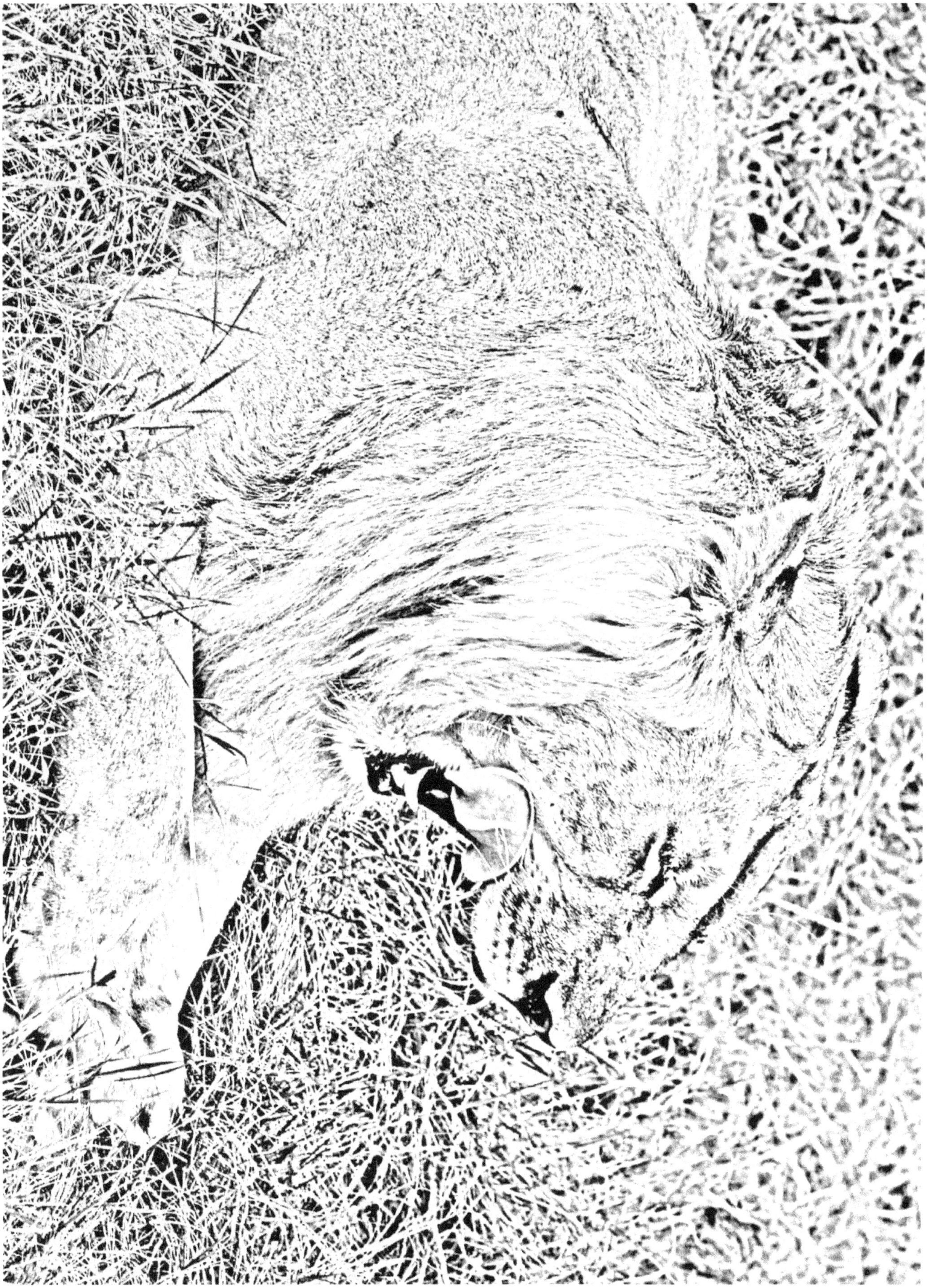

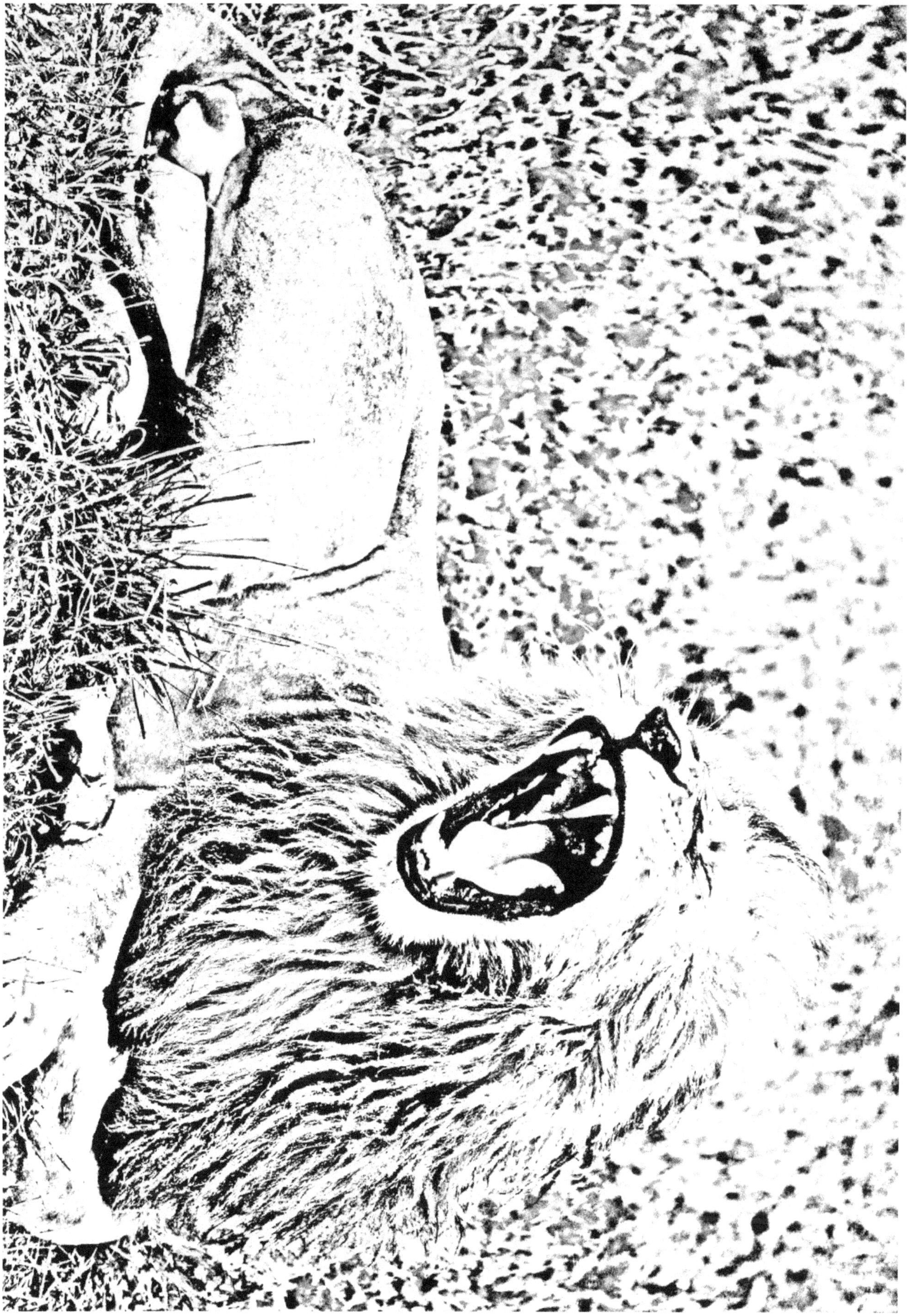

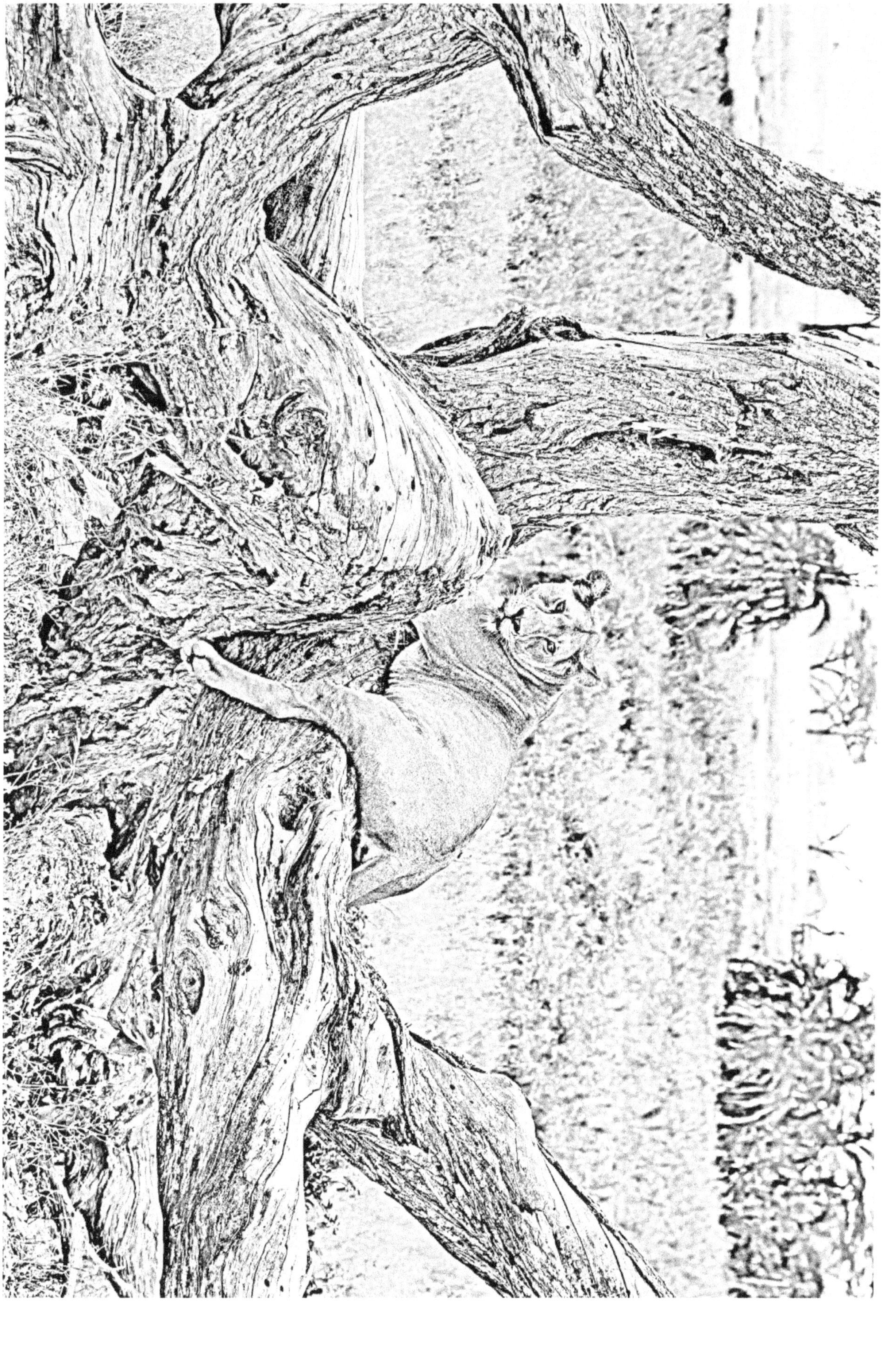

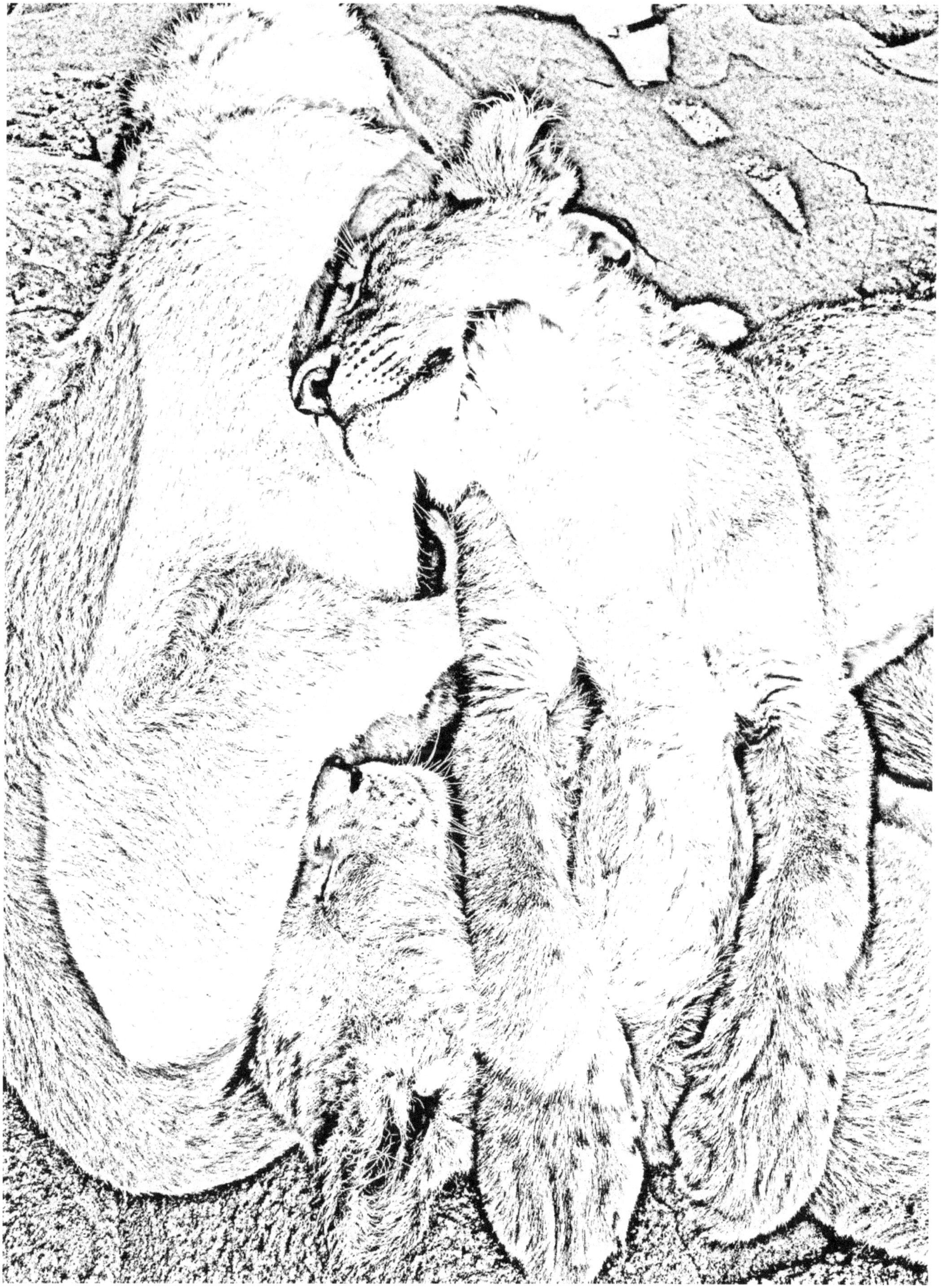

www.ingramcontent.com/pod-product-compliance
Lightning Source LLC
Chambersburg PA
CBHW080601180526
45168CB00007B/2732
9781515361947